MW01504551

YOU'RE BIG
and I'm Little
Let Freedom Ring!

YOU'RE BIG
and I'm Little
Let Freedom Ring!

P.K. Nelski

FirstPublish
A Division of the Brekel Group, Inc.
control your own destiny

Copyright © 19XX by P.K. Nelski.
All rights reserved. Printed in the United States of America.
No part of this publication may be reproduced, stored in
a retrieval system, or transmitted, in any form or by any
means, electronic, mechanical, photocopying, recording,
or otherwise, without the prior written permission of the
author.

ISBN
1-931743-22-3

Library of Congress Cataloging in Publication Data
2001119858

P.K. Nelski
You're Big and I'm Little, Let Freedom Ring

10 9 8 7 6 5 4 3 2 1

FIRSTPUBLISH
A Division of the Brekel Group Inc
300 Sunport Ln.
Orlando, FL 32809
407-240-1414
www.firstpublish.com

Thank You

I want to say a huge thank you to my husband, Dennis, for purchasing me my first computer, and for his **continual encouragement.**

I couldn't have completed this manuscript without the help from Shirley, my sister-in-law. She listened to me, night or day, on any brainstorm that I came up with.

Laurie, my sister, also gave me confidence to continue. She said, "If others can do it, you can too!" Thanks Laurie, those words never left my mind!

Special thanks to Justine, Esther, Ron, Ray, and Barry—for without their help, I don't know what I would have done.

And without Dr. Go, and his genuine care and expertise, I doubt if I would have had the strength to write this book. He is one in a million!

My mother-in-law, Lillian—who was the first to read this thing from cover to cover and gave me some good advice.

And last but certainly not least—appreciation for my children. Kirk, Melissa, Amanda and Eric who all listened to me while I pondered my next move to pursue my dream!

Oh yea thanks to my pooch. She was at my feet, the entire time I wrote this book!

Table of Contents

Preface

*A TRUE story of a fight to clear my name of identity
theft,
Involving one of the Dominant telephone providers in
the Midwest.*

$1.5 Million Dollars in fines awarded to Michigan,
THE GREAT LAKE STATE!

Identity theft is no laughing matter. It strips one of
their powers and causes many conflicts in ones life. With
computer accessibility and the Internet, personal identity
is being stolen much easier. This causes worry since
times are changing rapidly.

My story dates back to the year 1996 and has continued on to the present day. The energy trapped in my body
was bursting to come out. Warning the public became the
number one priority.

Here is the true story of how I stood up for my rights
as a consumer, on behalf of Michigan, and won. I have
learned to fight for what I believed in! I look back on it
now and I am thankful that I followed my heart.

Many other people wanted to know the details of the
proceedings. Writing a book seemed preferable over ver-
bally repeating the tale a billion times!

I feel as if 'I took a leap of faith' and found out not to
ask 'everyone' for their advice. Therefore, I didn't let
others stop me from what I knew was right. My autobiography, which is in its final edit stages, will be available

in the future. Due to personal reasons, beyond my control, I chose to hold off on its publication. That project was put on hold; thus my second book was started.

Some of the names have been changed in this story. Nicknames were given in place of their real identity. Basically, the 'names have been changed to protect the innocent'... and guilty. I wanted my story to be heard, but not at the risk of being hit any additional legal issues.

Thank you for taking the time to read about my story. I hope this book help others out somewhat. There is no doubt that it helped *me* to deal with the aftermath of it all.

God be with you,
Patricia Nelski

"Call to me and I will answer you." –Jeremiah 33:3
(The significance of this psalm will be realized later...)

Chapter 1

Surprise, Surprise!

I'll admit, it was a surprise when I found out that a Dominant Phone Provider had sent me to **two** collection agencies, for an account that I never had. You probably could have knocked me over with a feather! I was so angry that I began to cry. Could I fight another battle, like the one I fought a few years ago, involving the credit card scam? I thought 'it' was over! It just didn't seem fair that I was forced to fight to clear my name, *over* and *over* again.

I still believe, if it had not been for the telephone line that was opened in my name, the criminal could not have accomplished all that she did. She had a name, an address, a social security number and *now* a phone. It was obvious that she knew what she was doing.

Years back, approximately five years past, I was a victim of identity theft and fraud. I will try to share my experience with you. Hopefully, others that are going through a similar situation may find comfort in relating their story to mine. Maybe, just maybe, one can benefit from another's misfortune.

So with that said, I will try to tell the "David and Goliath" story, as referred to by a popular announcer for Channel UPN 50. (The day that the original story aired, 'David and Goliath' was used as a story prelude.) This made me chuckle! I felt as if I had made a difference, for at least the moment, and I felt a little proud. I'll remember this event for the rest of my life.

Going back to the beginning, I will say that the criminal was very experienced at her profession. The whole thing appeared to be easy for her to pull off. It certainly shocked the heck out of me and this is putting it mildly.

Committing the fraud seemed simple *once* she obtained ***the correct information.*** Of course, if the data did not match, it would have been rejected somewhere down the line, I think.

It didn't help matters that the Dominant Phone Provider had allowed this service to be opened in my name. Without a second piece of identification, or at the very least, *verifying* the social security number, a new account, in my name, was opened. By merely picking up the phone, inquiring about new service, then giving some information, she had herself a phone line! It sounds so simple, doesn't it?

The question was this…how could this have happened when the social security number she used was not correct and off by one digit? Regardless of this mistaken numeral, the account was granted and tagged to my name and credit report.

Another question was this…could she have opened the other lines of credit without an active, matching telephone? If the Dominant Phone Provider would have rejected her application, for service, could she have established the other fraud accounts? I doubt it. After working in an office setting you know the importance of obtaining a telephone number from your client. From a billing standpoint, the lending agent wants to know where they can contact you. Is an address enough? I don't care what anyone says, I think the telephone number played a major role in the fraud. Until I'm proven different, I'll continue to think that I am correct.

So in this case, my identity was *stolen*. Even though some of the information was inaccurate, she obviously had enough pieces to the puzzle, enabling her to imposter me. She did it so well, she chalked up $50,000 worth of credit card fraud in only a six-month period.

The **new** phone number along with the fraudulent address enabled her to obtain credit cards, (very easily), through the mail. Accounts were opened up in various cities, scattered all over the United States.

First of all, the DPP (the abbreviation that I'll use for Dominant Phone Provider), should have confirmed the request for service, with me, to see if I agreed with the new account. Affirmative action was not granted. I had not given the 'go-ahead with the new phone line' permission.

In addition to this, the DPP was guilty of another neglected procedure requirement. They failed to handle and resolve the conflict in a timely manner. How, after four years, could they come after me? None of it made sense. I mean, it wasn't even my social security number! Once again my rights as a consumer were blatantly violated.

I discovered the scam when my stepdaughter, Melissa, began flipping through the Yellow Pages. All of the sudden she said, "Pat, there's another one of you in the phone book, but she lives in another city!"

I answered her, in a tone of disbelief, "No way babe. There's not another one of me, in this world."

I glanced at the phone book and she was right! I couldn't believe my eyes! There *was* another one of "*me*" listed. I immediately got on the phone and called the DPP.

The DPP claimed that the account would be closed *immediately* and not to worry about it. I was promised that I would never see a bill, which I didn't. (They were right on that account!) Unfortunately, I took the DPP for their word and believed them. When they claimed that they had cleared my name, I truly believed them.

After discovering the "new" address in the phone book, I wrote to the credit reporting bureaus. I was scared that she had opened ***more than just a telephone*** in my name. I knew my credit was good and was seriously worried about my current credit status. I've heard a few stories of fraud happening to others, but you just don't think that it will happen to you.

It was the Fourth of July and our family made its way up north to celebrate Independence Day on the northern beaches of Michigan. I had to return home sooner than the rest, because I was scheduled to work for part of the holiday weekend. I left my family and drove home, by myself. Working at a home improvement warehouse involved rotating weekends. My job entailed managing contractors that were hired to install products that were purchased from my warehouse. (Doors, windows, plumbing, etc.)

My new husband, Dennis, kept the three children. In his care were K.J., who is my son and Melissa and Amanda, who are his daughters. The three of them were busy shooting off firecrackers and playing on the beaches in Charlevoix. As if it were preplanned, his two older sisters watched over K.J. and in no time at all were buddies. I sat thinking about the three of them and I knew they were having a good time together. I would have preferred to remain up north with my family, but I had to work.

The five-hour drive went by quickly and I was home before I knew it. As I pulled in our driveway, I grabbed the mail from the mailbox at the end of the driveway. A letter had arrived from one of the three credit reporting agencies in the United States. The envelope felt extremely thick, but since this was my first credit report, I didn't know that this was out of the ordinary.

I got out of the car, grabbed my duffel bag from the trunk and opened up the house. I stepped in; quickly looked around then walked back outside since it was a beautiful evening. My flowers were suffering from a severe case of the 'wilts', so I drenched them with water from the hose.

I then opened the letter that I had placed in my back pocket while I watered my Pink Impatiens. I was completely stunned at my credit report! Instead of it being a normal report, consisting of maybe three or four pages, mine was over twenty pages long!

I quickly flipped through the document and the more that I read, the more my hands began to shake! This couldn't be happening...I had never seen or even heard of the information that was being reported on me! Confusion, anger, and frustration were all rolled into one. There was $3,000 owed on a Visa to a bank in Virginia and another $2,500 to a Master Card in Ohio. These two, among many others, plagued my credit report making me appear as one low life individual instead of the hard working, honest person that I try to be.

The fraud list went on and on. My eyes quickly read the black writing on the white paper. I flipped through the pages thinking that *somehow* it was all just a big mistake. The more I read, the more upset I became.

I glanced next door to see if my neighbor's car was in the driveway and it was. I decided to go visit with Nancy—I needed someone to talk too. Maybe she could offer some advice about the mess that I appeared to be in.

I knocked on her door and when she opened it, she could see that I was trembling and that my eyes were filled with tears. I walked in, kicked off my shoes and handed her the papers that I had in my hand. She went to the refrigerator and grabbed a beer and handed it to me. I accepted the cold beer since it was a hot evening and I felt I could use a beer, or two. Nancy couldn't believe all of the information and agreed that it was mind-boggling. Trying to make sense out of it was a waste of time and was only infuriating me all the more. She was as shocked as I was.

It was frightening to think that something like this could happen, without one even knowing. In fact, if she had continued to make payments on the accounts, they'd *still* be running along smoothly, as if they were really hers ...that is, until she screwed up and missed payments. I'm quite confident this is what happened. It is apparent because some of the accounts had been active for almost a year. That's when they came looking for the 'real' Patty Nelski. (Will the real Patty Nelski please stand up?...ha...)

I felt totally helpless! It was a Saturday and a holiday weekend. It would have been impossible to make contact with anyone that could shed some light on my dilemma. I would have to *wait* until Monday before I could begin my investigation. (Not realizing, but this was the beginning *of a Six-Year Ordeal*.)

The following Monday, I immediately called our city's police department. They suggested that I call the Michigan State Police. Both of them said it "was out of their jurisdictions". (It seemed to be out of everyone's jurisdiction.)

I soon grew tired of hearing that excuse. The truth is, no one knew where to begin. *NO ONE* wanted to get involved since the crime was not committed in any *one* place. The fraudulent address resided in a city north of Monroe, Michigan. But since the accounts were creditors located from all over the United States, by mail, this made it impossible to find assistance. I guess *it really* wasn't *their* problem.

At one point, the frustration took over. Waiting around for some help became overwhelming so I decided to take the situation in my own hands. I got into my car and began my drive in search for the address that was listed as 'mine' on the credit report.

The anger began to build when I thought of what I would do when I finally met up with the person who did this to me. Once reaching the destination, I'd knock on the door and then what? I didn't know, but I was willing to find out.

My plan sort-of changed though. The person lived in an apartment located in a low-income complex that didn't look too friendly. After viewing the area I decided that my plan wasn't very smart. I appeared to be the minority, in that neighborhood and my Red Grand Am stuck out like a sore thumb!

Instead of knocking on the apartment in question, I decided to go to the local police department first. The suspect lived in their city and I felt confident that they would lend a helping hand. They HAD to help, didn't they? After all, the suspect lived in their city.

I walked in, and I asked to speak to the officer on duty. I introduced myself and gave him a brief synopsis of what had happened. I informed him that I had every intent on confronting the tenant then I asked to have a back up car follow me, just in case there was an altercation.

The officer listened to my plea for help and seemed to take me serious. I was left standing in the lobby while he walked through the locked door that led to the room behind the bulletproof glass. It wasn't long before I was asked to follow him to discuss the situation. I, too, was standing behind the bulletproof glass until I was offered a seat in front of the officer's desk.

I was informed that the suspect was a well-known female. She had a reputation for dealing in drugs and was dangerous. Therefore, I could be hurt and I was asked to let the law handle it. I was advised to stay away from her apartment. I should have guessed, another dead end!

At first, they seemed eager to help and assured me that the next time she was picked up, she'd be questioned. Hopefully, she would be caught with a fraudulent credit card, in my name. This would be the 'proof' that was needed. They would then have something to go on. Alone, my documents were not enough to act upon. I could tell by their reaction that they thought it was out of their 'jurisdiction' too.

They said that since the purchases were not made within the boundaries of their city, the law didn't lie within their hands. So the bottom line was this, the law hadn't been violated, (in their city). Were they passing the buck? Was this situation one they *should* have tried a little harder on? Or were they just as stumped as everyone else? I think they were stumped too.

I had just walked into another brick wall, another dead end. I had no choice but to forget about confronting her. I could only feel that, in time, the law would handle this situation for me. Reluctantly, I left, feeling defeated. Why didn't anyone seem to give a crap? SOMEONE, SOMEWHERE had to care!

I wrote to the President of the United States, out of complete desperation! I called the FBI and they were kind enough and spoke to me several times. The bottom line was fraud is not the responsibility of the Federal

Bureau of Investigation. Was I ever going to find an open door to help?

Finally, I decided to call a local Senator. I crossed my fingers and prayed he would care. At last, I was going to be given assistance and some relief. I was impressed with the concern and the prompt attention that I received. The Senator's office was the *first* to act upon this case of stolen identity and the United States Secret Service was notified. An agent was assigned to the case to investigate, almost immediately.

Then, to my surprise, a letter came responding to the one that I wrote to the President. They, too, made contact with the Secret Service, on my behalf. Since the fraud was over $15,000.00, the U.S. Secret Service was assigned to investigate...At last! Finally, when I felt as if I was at the end of my rope, someone was looking into the situation for me! I cannot describe how it felt to have the burden lifted from my shoulders. Although, the stress was overwhelming and not a day went by when I didn't contemplate the outcome.

Chapter 2

Maybe I Should Practice
My Typing Skills

Now that a formal investigation was underway, I began to focus my attention on the horrendous credit report. This is before my computer came along, so I began pecking away at my mom and dad's old typewriter, sitting in my makeshift office, at my kitchen table.

My sister, Laurie, stopped by to see how I was doing. She took a look at me and laughed. Since I was using an old time typewriter, I had typewriter ribbon ink smeared on my nose and chin. The wastebasket was at my side, which was slowly being filled with all of the 'errors' that I had crumbled into baseball sized trash. She went home, to return shortly thereafter, with a newer typewriter. It was still a manual version, but at least the letters didn't have that old fashioned shading within the "A's" and the "O's."

One by one, I wrote to each of the creditors listed on my credit report.

I can't tell you how many sheets of paper and correction fluid that I went through. I could see why I wasn't a secretary, with all of the mistakes I was making. Who would have guessed that I had typing in high school!

Each of the creditors made their demands. I was required to send identification and fill out an affidavit—a document that basically declares your innocence. The affidavit's were filled out and signed in front of a Notary of Republic, as a witness to your signature, swearing your innocence. In quite a few cases, the affidavits did not work and I still had calls coming in from the creditors on a regular basis.

Calls would come in on Sunday's or on the week nights, as late as nine o'clock. The caller would interrogate me, wanting to know 'when' I was going to pay the outstanding bills. I informed them that the accounts were not mine and that I had nothing to do with the opening of them. The callers were very rude and to top it all off, the caller would then hang up on me!

And 'they' say that I'm not the 'victim' here. ("They" being the credit bureau representatives.) They say that the 'taken creditors' are the victims. If the careless creditors wouldn't grant credit to just *any* name and social security number, this never would have occurred in the first place. How in the world was I **not** the victim? Could someone please explain this to me?

I continued to write letter after letter after letter. Finally, one of the creditors agreed to talk to me, in a normal voice. This woman told me that my impersonator went as far as to request a cash advance and the request was granted. A bank in Colorado Springs allowed the identity thief to forge my signature and then watch her sign her name under mine! She walked out of the bank with $1,500 in cash! A copy of the check was mailed to me, upon my request. How shocked I was to see my name forged by someone. Her handwriting did not resemble the real signature, in the least. She wrote it in cursive writing that slanted backward. My penmanship is rather nice and slants slightly forward. Besides that, she put 'S' down as a middle initial. My middle name is Kaye! (Named after a very special person in my life.) How could the bank be so stupid? And what was I going to do about it?

I thought about hiring an attorney and pressing charges. Unfortunately, not one attorney would even consider my case. The only advice I was given was that I should contact each creditor and tell them that the account was fraudulent. Well, I had already done this. Still, with this action already taken, no one was even remotely interested.

I was to learn that I was not alone in my struggle against identity theft. All agreed that something had to be done but no one knew where to begin. (Hopefully, by the time this book is published, I will have caused enough turmoil to change this.)

I was, no doubt, the victim and I felt truly helpless. I had worked very, very hard, after my divorce, to 'get out there' and make a good life for my son and I. I was married for six years before filing for divorce and was remarried within three years to Dennis.

The rage that I felt was, at times, unbearable. The situation was constantly on my mind. I'd go to sleep with it on my mind and I'd wake up and it would still be there. Somehow, someway I would make a difference in helping to stop this ever-growing problem. I didn't know what I was going to do, but I was going to do *something*! I just HAD TO!

Chapter 3

Arrested and Let Go! Can You Imagine That?

I continued to plug away with my letter writing. I kept all of the correspondence and my pile of information grew. Laurie came over with a carrying case that she had picked up at a garage sale for me. It was made of leather and resembled a big envelope, only it closed with a push latch. It was stuffed to the max in no time at all.

With every letter that I composed, the writing became a bit easier. I eventually became proficient at my newest task at hand. I was able to speed up my process, with all of the practice that I was getting.

It was not easy to work and take care of my family AND fight this battle. Although, my determination remained strong and I refused to give in. It seemed as if I was composing a letter, every other day. I was determined that **no one** would ruin my credit record, not after all of my hard work to maintain an excellent credit status. Approximately one year later, my efforts paid off. My credit report became spotless, once again.

Even with my credit report back to normal, I wanted to confront the person who had caused this nightmare. She deserved to be in jail behind bars. She was destroying my life and the lives of my family. Friends purposely stayed away because they were sick of listening to me. I was confused...why didn't anyone seem to care about trying to arrest her? Wasn't this a big enough case to bother with or what?

Feeling discouraged, I called my Secret Service Agent. I know I was bugging them but if I kept quiet I knew my case would be on the back burner. My agent was always polite when I spoke with her regarding the issue. She informed me that they were waiting for the suspect to resurface, since she went into hiding. I grew impatient but tried to remain thankful that I had an agent acting on my behalf.

I could tell by my credit report that she fled from her home, here in Michigan, to a residence in Florida. (The current credit report listed another address for 'me'. How this angered me...I obviously did not live in Florida!)

I called up my agent to tell her about *my* 'detective' discovery. At times, it felt as if I was doing the legwork in locating her. I tried to accept this, since I was sure things were prioritized. Obviously, the Secret Service had many other things to consider besides Patty Nelski, in Michigan, who was doing her best to be a thorn in somebody's side. Otherwise, I would have been filed away, in a forgotten folder, for perhaps indefinitely. I wanted her to be arrested and justice served! I wanted this over, once and for all.

A call came in, one afternoon, and to my surprise the criminal was finally apprehended and brought back to Michigan to stand trial! I was ecstatic! Hooray! I'd sing quietly to myself..."***She's going to jail!***"

Little did I know that I was *completely* wrong. She **did** go in front of the judge but 'due to the unwillingness of the credit card companies to supply the necessary data needed to prosecute,' *she was let go*! HOW COULD THIS HAPPEN?

Our system failed me and justice was not served. I was let down, to say the least. To this day, she is still walking free, to do it again to another innocent victim. (At least to my knowledge.) I began to wonder how many other times that she had committed the same type of fraud, over the last five years. How many other lives had she screwed up...

I tried, the best I knew how, to draw attention to the problem. Now I had to face the cold, hard fact. She was a "free" woman—not punished in the slightest. She had a slap on the wrists and set free. It made me wonder just what was up with our world.

After writing to many people, calling television studios and visiting the local newspaper, I still couldn't believe that someone was capable of stealing my identity! How could I not have known about it? If it could happen to me, it could happen to anyone, and it just wasn't fair. I wanted to warn the public and to be aware, for she was still out there, somewhere.

Channel 50 was called and they showed up at my house with their camera crew. After a brief segment on the evening news, I received a call and was asked if I would attend a meeting in Lansing, Michigan's Capital. A Privacy Hearing was scheduled with five of our Senators. The meeting was to discuss the fraud issue and to consider changes in our system to try to prevent future problems.

My drive to Lansing made me feel like I was doing all that I could do. I was pleased that I was going to get a chance to talk. At the hearing I was assured that a Privacy Issue was in front of Congress and steps were being be taken to fight back against identity theft. (This was February 12th, 1997.)

Once again, I had to turn this problem over to God. I had my family to care for along with the every day problems that life presents. Therefore, my feet had to remain on the ground, some of the time. I did some soul searching and knew that *someday justice would one day be served.* Perhaps not in this world, but in the world to come, since someday, she would have to *meet her maker*.

Chapter 4

"IT'S B-A-C-K!"

L ife was rolling along relatively normal. We had moved into our new home and had sold the one in Southgate. No longer did I smell the fumes or hear the roar of the automobiles traveling along the expressway. The noise pollution was replaced by the sound of hundreds of chirping birds.

Living in the woods can be rather peaceful and quite serene. I slowly adjusted to country life…without a neighbor right next to me. The nearest resident is over on the next five-acre parcel and we're living on a ten-acre lot. We moved just in time to see the colorful fall leaves. There was no doubt that the winter chill was in the air.

I decided to check out the mall near our new home and begin my Christmas shopping. The hard part came in when I had to keep the gifts until the actual holiday! (I have a hard time keeping secrets!) I was between jobs and I thought it would be better if I could do most of my shopping at one store. I would charge them, and pay it off, right after Christmas.

At one of my favorite department stores, my credit limit was rather low, due to my prior request. I was afraid to have too much credit accessible, just in case my information was stolen again. Since my credit limit was modest, I thought an increase would make my shopping that much easier. And *this* is when IT all began again.

I met Cassie, a sales clerk in the children's department. I was the only person in her line, which allowed us to talk. I inquired about an increase on my credit card limit and she offered to take care of it for me, while I waited.

I told her about the fraudulent phone line that was opened years earlier. I then went on to explain about the fifteen other creditors who were harassing me for payment on accounts that I never had. Fifty Thousand dollars of credit card fraud is a lot of money when you stop to think about it. It is hard to remain calm when it's your life and finances that are being screwed with.

Cassie was put on hold, for quite some time, while the credit department conducted their investigation. I feared that something was wrong. The scenario was all too familiar. I told her, "Oh no…it's starting all over again! I'm not sure if I can do this again! I've been declined credit so many times; I've actually lost count!"

The embarrassment began to build since I was no longer the only customer waiting in line. I could hear the whispers of others while they grew impatient. I began to receive strange looks from the other women, after all, I was holding up the line. Cassie didn't seem to mind their impatience though.

My happy go lucky; Christmas shopping mood was abruptly changed into anger when my credit was declined. Due to the derogatory information being reported on my report, the increase could only be minimal. It 'looked' as if I had failed to pay my bills once again. I could feel the glare coming from the others that had been waiting. I felt as big as an ant.

Cassie was kind and listened to me. I quickly advised her on the importance of keeping her social security number, *extremely* private. She was a lot younger than I, probably still in high school. Maybe she would benefit from what I had learned the hard way. I told her not to trust anyone when it came to her information.

She wished me luck on the book that I was writing. After promising her a copy of it, someday, I left the mall. My Christmas spirit was now gone and feeling rather depressed instead. It looked as if another battle was beginning and to be truthful...I wasn't in the mood to fight anymore. I felt that I had been burning my candle at both ends and one day the ends were going to meet.

I wrote for a current issue of my credit report and tried to prepare myself for what awaited me. Credit reports can take as long as six weeks to receive, so I tried not to worry too much. Christmas has always been special to me, and I wasn't going to let this ruin it for my family and I. My new report wouldn't arrive until after the New Year, so I forced the thoughts from my head.

The public was hyped up on Y2K. Was it all going to end at midnight anyway? I didn't think so, but I'll admit that I felt some apprehension. (Yes, I had a few bottles of water on hand, just in case.)

Chapter 5

Another Answered Prayer!

Christmas came and went, and it was enjoyed as much as usual. I absolutely LOVE Christmas! There have been times when I've made *so many* purchases and had *so many* packages that I was literally stuck in the middle of the mall, pondering my next move. How was I going to carry all of the gifts and why did I buy so much?

The long awaited credit report finally showed up in February. It was not as bad as the one that I received years earlier, but the same anger came rushing back. How could the DPP send me to two collection agencies for an account that was never mine? The seemingly incompetence made me wonder how many others were in my shoes?

Since the phone was opened in my name, with the incorrect social security number, how could they just 'throw' it under my name and number? Now **this** had to be against the law! I began to cry. I wasn't ready for this again. I knew, from before, that it was going to be a struggle. My heart began to pound and it felt as if would pop out of my chest.

I called Dennis at work and he tried to calm me down, but it didn't work. I hung up the phone and sat on the floor in the kitchen and cried more. (This may sound strange, but unless you've been there, you will not understand this feeling.) You're incapable of 'fixing' the problem and you're at the mercy of someone else. I asked God for help since I needed *his* guidance.

Finally, my tears subsided and I began to make a few phone calls. Trying to get a hold of any one at the DPP who knew what they were doing was impossible. This only frustrated me all the more.

Somehow, I managed to get in touch with a woman who worked for the City of Detroit in its Consumer Affairs Division. Her name was Justine Smith and I had finally met a caring individual who would remain by my side.

Justine listened to my story and felt confident that she could help me. She had been dealing with a cooperative DPP representative regarding other identity theft victims. She was sure that the matter would be taken care of efficiently, once the representative was informed of the mishap.

Sitting on the living room floor, I began sorting through my documents. This is when I realized the importance of a paper trail. If I had failed to file the documents away for future use, I wouldn't have had the proof that I would need.

Hours went by while I carefully reviewed all that I kept over the years. Letters that were written and ones that I received and tons of credit reports going back to the beginning.

Spiral notebooks were filled with dates and events and conversations that took place over the course of the past five years.

I photocopied all pertinent documents and then immediately put them in the mail for her to review. This is when I began to keep all receipts for postage. A few bucks here and a few bucks there and before you knew it, the money really added up.

Justine phoned a few days later to say that she had received my bundle of 'proof'. She was perplexed that this entire event had taken place and it was quite unbelievable! Her eagerness to assist me was comforting and she commended me on my excellent record keeping. I definitely had a large pile of papers that was growing with each passing day. This would end up being evidence—my 'proof' that it all took place.

Later that week, the facts were placed in the hands of the DPP representative. A letter of reassurance arrived in the mail. The matter was now under control. Their final accounts department was notified and within ninety days, the account would be removed from my credit report.

I was elated that it was solved, so easily this time. I would not miss the inevitable battle that I was sure I was faced with again. I could live with the ninety-day guideline! Boy, was I glad that I came across Justine!

I took a few moments to compose a note expressing my appreciation. Her supervisor was notified and my thank you was heard. I must say, it was a pleasure composing a letter using gratifying words, commending one on a job well done instead of expressing anger.

Feeling confident that 'it' was over, normal life rolled on. I hadn't heard any news either way, so the cliché 'no news was good news' prevailed in my mind. It wasn't until ten or eleven months later when I discovered that I was wrong, once again. (This was just another twist in the struggle for innocence.) I was declined a car loan and numerous other lines of credit. My report wasn't restored at all...in fact; I was to find out that the DPP had done nothing, nothing at all! I had to face reality—this was never going to end, was it?

Justine called and sounded disappointed to discover that the DPP had failed her too. I started to re-think the chance of hiring an attorney. Once again, numerous attempts were made. But the response was the same. Hiring an attorney was *still* a dead end. No one had even the slightest desire to consider a case against the phone giant. They were all 'chicken.'

Years had passed since the original, breathtaking, day and **WE** were no closer to solving this Nation's identity theft crisis. Although, one thing did change...statistics had shown that the number of fraud cases were piling up at an alarming rate.

The next day we had a break through! The phone rang and it was Justine. She wanted to know if I'd mind if the Michigan Public Service Commission, in Lansing, reviewed my paperwork? Did I mind? I'd be elated!

I kept thinking of the woman who did this to me— where was she living at? Comfortably in Florida, enjoying the sun and possibly doing the same thing to other people?

How I wished I had a crystal ball to gaze into... I wanted to confront her and, just out of curiosity, see what she looked like. And what would I do if I saw her? Maybe clobber her with a wooden chair...

Chapter 6

Sorry to Bore You With this Chapter!

The whole situation was starting to wear me down. It was as if I was beating my head against a brick wall. I spent so much energy 'thinking' only to end up with a migraine. It's as if you're running but not moving an inch.

My health was declining at a rapid rate. I had a severe case of indigestion and the burning in my throat was constant. I ate 'Tums' by the handful, but they did not phase me. I drank 'Mylanta' and even resorted to drinking a mixture of baking soda and water. The baking soda caused a much-needed burp and relief, momentarily, but soon the unbearable burning returned. My stomach ached continually and the burning in my throat was relentless.

Finally, I convinced my doctor, (the one that I had at this time), that I needed more information on my condition. I've never had the misfortune of heartburn. I finally asked her, "Do you think maybe it's time for a few tests?" (With a managed health care network, obtaining a referral was like pulling teeth.)

An Upper GI was done and I was diagnosed with having 'Acid Reflux' disease. When I had the procedure performed, the technician let me watch the television screen during the procedure. I could see why I hurt in my throat. After swallowing the Barium, I watched it make its way to my stomach. Then, immediately, it changed direction.

The X-ray allowed the Barium to be visible and it appeared as if it were a fluorescent snake, traveling back up into my throat. Was that why it hurt when I ate? The stuff was coming back up and wasn't staying in the stomach, where it belonged?

My nerves were getting the best of me and I knew it; but I was having a hard time 'getting through' to my physician. She appeared to be very closed minded, or something, and didn't listen to me. She knew about my personal dilemma and didn't seem to understand.

I became alarmed when my weight began to drop. First, just a few pounds here and there, but then my clothes made it obvious that I was becoming a skeleton. I needed help! But where was I going to get it? I mean, my *own* doctor didn't believe me. You would think that the drop in weight alone would have sent up a red flag! It wasn't like I had any weight to spare. I begin to wonder if I am the crazy one, after all?

Soon, I stopped eating altogether because it hurt too bad. Even with the rapid weight loss, nothing was done. I was simply given a prescription that would prevent the formation of the excess stomach acid. A bland diet was suggested and I was to sleep with my head elevated.

None of this worked! My energy level was very low and I lost over ten pounds and was weighing in around one hundred and two. (I am five foot and four inches tall.) I began drinking 'Ensure' to provide calories and consuming 'Gatorade.'

All of this was extremely out of character for me. Normally I'd be buzzing around like a little red headed tornado, never stopping to sit, until bedtime. Now, my energy was gone. I sat around alot and sleep was difficult due to the burning in my throat. At night, the house would be quiet, the rest of the family asleep; but, I'd be up walking around, trying to find relief from the stomach pain and awful burning.

Even with my efforts to regain strength, it felt as if I was fighting a losing battle. The conflict was taking its toll on me and was causing me more harm than just to my credit status. It felt as if my nerves were actually killing me!

It was obviously time for a second opinion and I'm not sure why I kept procrastinating. It was plain to see that my physician and I were getting no where, fast. She didn't have a clue as to what I was feeling inside. (Once again, unless you've been a victim of identity theft—I'm not sure if you can fully understand.)

It was a Saturday and Dennis and I had just gotten into a squabble. (It wasn't that bad of an argument, but when you feel weak, any argument is one too many.) I couldn't take **any** more crap, from anyone. I was getting weaker by the day and I complained a lot. The drinking of the 'liquid dinners' wasn't helping with the weight problem.

I *finally* called my doctor's office and was surprised to find a physician scheduled on the weekend. The receptionist listened and was able to squeeze me into the schedule for later that afternoon. Maybe, just maybe, someone would finally help me!

I have to admit—I looked lawful. My face was as white as a ghost and I had dark circles under my eyes. I would have made a good-looking ghoul if it had been around Halloween. To top it all off, people were asking if I was an Anorexic!

My new doctor overheard me talking to the nurse while she took my blood pressure. She asked the usual questions…. You know, what are your symptoms? Where do you hurt? Etc.? She couldn't believe that the problem had been going on for as long as it had been.

Then, Dr. Benedict Go walked in and I knew he'd help me, or at least prayed to God that he would. This may sound drastic, but *felt as if I was I slowly dying*. I wasn't in control of gaining my weight back. My energy level was so low; I was out of breath continually.

Dr. Go came to my rescue and I know that I was meant to meet him! He is the one responsible for my upward climb towards recovery. Soon my health began to improve dramatically. I would finally feel as if I was on the right track.

Fate intervened for me, on this particular Saturday, and I felt that I was meant to go to the doctor's office. You see, Dr. Go alternates with his physician colleagues and works every fifth Saturday. It just so happened that it was his turn to work, therefore an appointment was made with him instead of my normal doctor.

When I explained about the fraudulent phone line and the fifty thousand dollars worth of debt that I was dealing with, he was appalled! *Ironically enough*, he had been a recent victim of identity theft also! The fraud committed in Dr. Go's name was only five thousand dollars, not fifty thousand, but he could relate to the frustration that I was feeling. He had fought his own battle and was able to clear his own credit. He agreed that it was all very nerve wrecking.

He admitted that the stress he experienced was difficult to handle and could see why my health was poor. My nerves were the reason for the demise to my health. When you're all nerved up, your body makes an excessive amount of adrenaline and a weakening to your immune system. This makes it difficult for your body to heal itself or fight infection.

He sat down and actually *listened* to me. His friendly attitude was a pleasant surprise and was welcomed wholeheartedly! Dr. Go was calm and took quite a bit of time with me and it was obvious that he would help me through this ordeal. A scope of my stomach was ordered since my symptoms were severe. He wanted to see if I had an ulcer.

I believe him when he said that the stress **was** causing the physical ailment. We had to get the stress under control before the rest of me could heal. I had an excess of amount of acid in my stomach, that would eventually travel back up the esophagus. That is why the burning sensation never left. My weight loss had to stop and my fluid intake had to increase.

From that day forward, not only did I have a new doctor, but a true friend. A doctor is supposed to *listen to you* as well as prescribe medicine. If they don't listen, then how can they diagnose and treat you correctly?

P.K. Nelski

Two weeks later, I was feeling well enough to type my new doctor a thank you letter. Just a simple note was sent, for the care that I received. I regret not changing to a new physician sooner, but who knows, I may have not chosen him!

My turning point had finally arrived and my positive attitude began to reemerge. I was usually an optimist...and the optimist had returned. My stomach slowly regained stability and my overall well being was healthier. I was finally getting relief from feeling like a 'walking battery.' When 'they' say stress can almost kill you, 'they' aren't kidding.

Chapter 7

Does Worrying Run in Our Family or What?

Soon, I was to receive a call from Justine. The Public Service in Lansing had completed their review of my documents and asked if I'd consider testifying against the DPP. (Testifying for the violations of the Michigan Telecommunications Act.) If I won, I'd have a chance to make changes in the way the current system is run. If I lost, then it would have been well worth the effort.

I was warned that this was going to be tough, but I knew I could not turn them down. Even if it meant a set back in my health, I had to act on the opportunity at hand. I'd just have to take that chance, wouldn't I? I immediately answered with a firm but anxious, "YES!"

I was nervous about testifying and I began to receive calls from the DPP, trying to convince me that going to court was not needed. It was a little too late to negotiate, as far I was concerned. When I wanted to talk to someone when the problem began, no one was available. Now, all of the sudden, there was a sense of urgency, on their part. They were calling me to discuss the situation.

Although, they did stop after I told them that I was going through with the testimony. Well, I wasn't going to turn back. I was finally going to get to tell my story and maybe, just maybe, someone would listen!

I also began therapy with a Guidance Center. It felt strange admitting that I needed someone to talk too. I had plenty of friends but soon they and the family grew sick of hearing me ramble on about the problem that continued to plague me. The sad part about it was it wasn't only happening to me, but also to them since they had to listen to the same story over and over.

I often spoke of the hearing, against the DPP. It was coming up soon and I was nervous. On the outside, I tried to act tough, but on the inside, I felt queasy. This 'worrying' was supposed to have been stopped, since I knew it wasn't good for my stomach.

Dennis and I had our share of arguments too. I'm **sure** it was hard to live with me. The family was used to the 'Patty' who was light hearted and funny. Not this negative, depressed person who couldn't complain enough.

Now that my stomach was getting slowly better another ailment flared up. When all this stress came down originally, my heart also reacted to the continual fretting. When I first discovered my credit nightmare, the original shock was the worst to adjust to. The initial helplessness was heartrending. I experienced chest pain while my left arm turned purple. One medical personnel said it was because my shirt was too tight. Yea right! How come it happened when I was naked?

I went to the emergency room and tests were ordered. The diagnosis was a Mitral Valve Prolapse. (Which is actually quite common.) As the blood flows, your heart is beating and the valve is supposed to shut, in between the beats. The blood then continues to pump forward through the heart. The valve is defective, which is allowing some of the blood to regurgitate, or flow backward.

Daily heart medication entered my life. I was placed on a hefty dose, to be taken both at morning and at night. My actual heart was still good though. If the valve would stop flopping around, I would be just fine. I guess the floppiness is what caused the pain. My arm stopped turning blue, after beginning the medication. Someday, I may have to face the fact that I'll undergo surgery for a replacement valve.

I've always heard that stress can cause all kinds of problems and now I believe it. I know we all have the stresses of every day living in our lives. So who in the world needs the 'extra' crap? The bottom line is, I had to try to stay calm through the hearing process.

In the beginning, the Michigan Public Service tried to talk me out of going through with it. They knew I was already experiencing health difficulties and this would probably have an adverse effect on my well being. I was told that it was okay to accept an offer from the DPP and forget about the testifying, especially if it was going to affect me adversely. They said that someone else would eventually come along and follow through with the legal proceedings. My friends at the Public Service Commission cared for me.

Well, I can say that I was warned but I chose to go forward. Nothing ventured, nothing gained...(my mom always said that to me when I was younger.) THERE

WAS NO WAY OF ME BACKING DOWN——not unless I died first! I was finally going to be heard! In the years earlier, if someone would have taken the time to just listen… maybe none of this court room crap would be taking place.

My therapist, Carmen, was a great help to me. Instead of driving my family crazy, I drove her crazy instead. My health care provider agreed to cover twenty visits a year. I eventually began seeing, Dr. Kubrak, one of the doctors on staff at the clinic. He logically explained that my feelings of anger, hurt, and wanting justice to be served were all normal feelings. Somehow, I did feel better after talking with him. Although, I still hated to admit that I had to receive psychiatric counseling, but their course of treatment helped to keep the stress level tolerable. Therapy was a wise move and I'm glad that I had enough sense to take the steps toward help. I just reached out and asked.

Another physician of mine has proven to be a special kind of guy. I've been fortunate to have a 'mentor', at my side—never too busy to listen. Therefore, I must mention my dear friend and Chiropractor, Dr. Russell. He's been my physician for eight years and has kept me walking. I had a previous injury while employed as a truck driver involving my discs in my spine. *(But this is truly another story.)* Dr. Russell has a gifted quality to somehow make you feel special, just when you need it most. His office managers, Dawn and Nancy have been a sounding board, displaying the same caring disposition.

While I'm mentioning the medical personnel in my life, I must add that I've had the same Gynecologist for fourteen years! I'll continue to be Dr. Bernal's patient for as long as I can! I've been blessed with superior physicians and a bond of trust has been established.

Chapter 8

The Strange Phone Call

The DPP was calling my house trying talk me into settling. I was repeatedly informed that my name would be cleared. Why should I believe them now? Hadn't I heard that before?

Each day, I'd enter the house, after running an errand or two and see the answering machine blinking. Numerous attempts were made on their part to make contact, but I had no intent on settling out of court.

After ignoring them for days, the phone rang and, for some reason, I decided answer it, instead of letting the answering machine screen the call. The person on the line asked to speak to "Patricia". I *knew* it had something to do with the case and something inside warned me to beware. I had a strange feeling.

I said, "Can I put you on hold for just a second?"

He answered politely, "Sure. I can wait."

I had to regain my composure and try to talk without sounding too anxious or concerned. I wanted to sound professional. Instead of speaking into the handset, I utilized the speaker format of the phone so the voice echoed throughout the room.

He introduced himself and to my surprise, he was the judge who was assigned to the case involving the DPP and I. He went on to say how *things like this* are preferred to be handled out of court.

First of all, I didn't like the sound of *things like this...*

I was quite confused and asked, "Aren't you supposed to be a neutral party? Why are you calling me?"

He answered, sounding a little shocked at my bluntness, "Patricia, will you at least agree to talk to the DPP?"

I snapped back, this time allowing the tone of my voice to reflect my emotion. I said, "You don't understand, do you? I have every intent on testifying."

A silence came over the line. It seemed like forever and I hadn't heard a peep from the caller. I finally broke the silence with, "Hello.....are you still there?"

At last he answered a moment later, with an even more shocked reply, "Can you please repeat that last statement?"

What part of it didn't he understand? I slowly and distinctly began to repeat myself, "I said that I have every intent on testifying against the DPP. They are very wrong, therefore I do not wish to discuss this matter with them. And I do not want their money. I want their procedures changed. But I thank you for your call." (I didn't want to sound rude, since I didn't know if this *was* a common practice.)

I don't mean to accuse anyone here, but the call was strange! I hung up the phone and called Dennis at work and explained the conversation to him. He also thought that the request was out of the norm. Maybe it was okay for one to try to 'intervene', to save on court costs. I hung up the phone with my husband and immediately dialed Justine.

I didn't waste any time. This made me feel as if the cards were stacked against me, right from the start. After talking to Justine, I dialed Esther and Ron. They were working together on my case, at the Public Service Commission. It was apparent that they accomplished alot together and I could sense their efficiency. They were *truly a **Godsend!***

Others seemed to be equally concerned about the recent event. I can't say for sure what the intent was, but it just didn't seem <u>right</u> to me. Nothing much was said about this strange occurrence and I too dropped it. Luckily, the judge was dismissed from the case and a new one was assigned. The court date that was already on the calendar was crossed out and a new one was penciled in. It was rescheduled for one month. Another month to wait and ponder the outcome.

Chapter 9

The Tornado Came Close

The night before the first hearing was a very bizarre evening. The storm was predicted, so we knew it was on its way, but it hit faster than anticipated. If I'm not mistaken, the original weather forecast called for only thunderstorms with occasional lightening strikes not an actual tornado warning.

I wasn't alarmed, though, since I am one of those people who are mesmerized by nature and the power of God in action. Perhaps the lack of fear comes from my upbringing. My mom would remain calm during the midst of a storm. Although she would make us three girls get in the hallway. If the weather became too fierce, she would order all of us to get under a mattress that was placed in the narrow walkway. (We kept a cot mattress stored under one of the twin beds, which was frequently used when a friend slept over.)

For some reason, it seemed like the majority of the bad weather would strike around dinnertime. And my dad would not be home from work yet then I would become worried of his whereabouts.

I'd ask my mom, "Do we have to get in the hallway yet?" I would have preferred to stand on the front porch and witness the raging wind! (It still amazes me to *stand still and just watch.*)

Although, I can remember this one particular storm and my dad was home—my sisters and I felt sorry for the tree in our front yard. We begged him to 'go help it'. So that is what he did. My father would have done anything for his girls. He went out to the garage and came back out with three or four stakes, a hammer, and a ball of rope. The stakes were pounded into the ground around the trunk of the tree. The ropes were attached to the trunk and with the help of the stakes, kept the tree intact and upright. My dad saved our tree.

Did you ever notice that the birds' even know when something's up? They actually become silent too! (At least, here in our woods they do.) You know that nature isn't fooling around when the gusts of wind stop and the tops of the trees decide to stand still. It's almost as if the leaves are forbidden to make even the slightest rustle. One could almost hear a pin drop.

An eerie feeling takes over and the silence seems to linger in the air heavily. I heard that if, at the break of the silence, you suddenly hear something that resembles a freight train, you may be in the path of a tornado. Now I don't know if this is fact or myth, so don't quote me on it. If I ever live to find out first hand, I'll be sure to mention it.

The eerie feeling intensifies; then, it's as if God turns on a huge, high-powered fan. The trees begin to rock back and forth, again. At first, slowly, but then the gentle swaying emits more energy with each passing moment. Soon, they look as if they've engaged in an aerobic workout, trying to perform backbends, testing the integrity of their trunks. The greenish sky turns a deeper shade of pea green. This is when one should run for cover...or at least order their child too.

That's what happened the night before the first hearing. I was working quickly, waiting to the last minute to get ready, as usual. I ironed my clothes while making dinner, in between the intervals of basting the turkey breast that was roasting in the oven.

I continued to type, ignoring my son's pleas to stop. I was trying, my best to make an opening statement that would grab the attention of the others in the courtroom. I have a tendency to get sidetracked and I knew I had to be completely, 100% professional. So, if I was going to make any sense at all, I had to prepare a dialog to follow.

Of course, I ran into obstacles. What wording sounded better? What would an attorney say? Shirley, my sister-in-law, and a wonderful friend of mine came to the rescue, once again. She lives up north, in God's country, way up high on a hill, with a view that is breathtaking. (Shirley lives in East Jordan, very close to the home we had, in Charlevoix.)

Luckily, for me, Shirley worked for an attorney some year's back. (I found out that we do live in a small world. To my surprise, the attorney that she was employed with was the same attorney that my first husband and I sought advice from, years ago. Then, when I met her, after my first date with Dennis, I realized why Shirley looked so familiar to me!)

I phoned Shirley, for the fifth time that day. Somehow, she could always make my normal everyday words sound more professional. I quickly read her what I had composed and awaited her advice.

The wind began to batter things around outside. A lawn chair went tumbling away from our home and landed at the edge of the woods. Large branches began to fall from the trees surrounding our house. Garbage cans tipped over emptying their contents on the ground.

Our new home had a lot of windows, along the back of the house. The view of the woods and all of nature is very clear. The living room appeared to be rather "green", but I chose to ignore it. K.J. was keeping me posted, minute by minute, as he stayed tuned to the television. He would read, out loud, the warning as it scrolled across the bottom of the screen. It was time to take cover.

I was too busy expressing my thoughts. I read what I had typed on the computer screen, to Shirley, not taking a moment to look up long enough to pay attention to the weather. K.J. would complain *"MOM*, get off of the computer... there's a bad storm coming.... *Mom...!"*

Shirley could hear the complaining and she asked, "Is it really that bad there, Pat? You should hit *print* now!"

I ignored Shirley momentarily while I turned to K.J. and said, "Honey, go get in the basement...I'm almost done here.... just another second or two." At Shirley's demand, I finally printed what I had on file, typo's and all. Then 'Bam'...my computer crashed. The electricity went out and we were suddenly left in the dark. Out here in the woods, when it gets dark, I mean it gets DARK.

We don't have streetlights and there's not a neon sign for miles.

K.J. exclaimed, "I told you mom! "

I replied, "You're right and I was completely wrong! It *is* sort-of spooky outside, isn't it?" I stood up slowly and pushed the chair up to the roll-top desk. All of the sudden I heard the front door creak. (I was thankful for the fine job my husband did when he installed that door –hopefully with a few extra screws! Somedays, when the sun is first rising in the morning, the rays shine through the leaded glass and illuminate the house with intricate shapes.) The door began to creak again, this time, slightly louder.

I said, "Did you hear the door creak? It sounds as if it could blow right in and send me off through that picture window."

K.J. looked at me and said, "You're not afraid, are you mom? Get out of the way, just in case!"

I moved out of the walkway and went around the house gathering the dozens of candles that we had. Thank goodness for those candles and the two flashlights with batteries that actually worked.

I was nervous for the following morning and I really wanted to look as good as possible for the hearing. Now, with the power outages, not only did I fail to complete my paperwork, I would not be able to shower and curl my hair the following morning, as planned. (When I wake up in the morning, I have a serious case of 'bed head'!)

I sat by candle light, feeling like an old time writer. All I needed was the feather quill tip pen dipped into ink. I had a mission, with or without the help of Thomas Edison, although electricity would have made my writing a little easier.

Come to find out, a tornado did touch down very, very close to our house.

Less than five miles away, a huge tree was uprooted and dropped onto the neighbors' front porch. It seemed as if someone did not want me to testify.

Dennis came to my rescue though. He pulled up our motor home, close to the house, so I could use the generator. So, at five o'clock in the morning, I started it up and was able to get ready after all!

The drive to Lansing was a little creepy too. Power lines were down, so some of the intersections were without traffic lights. Trees were scattered all over the expressway, not just branches—actual trees. I think I should have taken cover, the previous night. Maybe, I learned my lesson, in that area anyway.

Chapter 10

I Can Look Like an Attorney Too!

At the initial meeting with their attorney, I felt I was on equal ground with him. It didn't matter to me that he had years of college behind him. He came into court with a suit and tie—like anyone else that was dressed up. I mean, he could have been in sales for that matter.

I showed up in my suit too. I figured that a new outfit was called for. I had to look like I knew what I was doing anyway. I bought a navy blue suit with satin lapels. It was rather modern, but conservative at the same time. The important thing was this; I had to feel good in it. Well, the suit was comfortable so I strolled into court, that morning, filled with confidence.

I was a little nervous when I introduced myself and extended my right hand to my opponent. His palm felt sweaty and I noticed that perspiration began to bead on his forehead. Could he be more nervous than I was? He appeared to be rather inexperienced. Actually, he seemed like a nice enough guy. I would bet that he was younger than I though.

The courtroom was called to order and the judge began with asking each of us to name our position along with our title. The introductions began, starting with the State of Michigan's counsel. Esther took her turn, then mine was next. Great...what would I say? "Patricia Nelski and I don't have a title at the moment..."My turn came up faster than I had hoped. I proudly and with careful articulation pronounced my name, "Patricia Nelski and I am acting on my own behalf."

The introductions continued along to the DPP's staff. My mind wandered off and something didn't seem *right*——There was one person that I felt was missing up there with us. This person had already helped many people...this person was Ron. He had been my knowledgeable friend and what do you know, he didn't even get to say his name.

I think this was the first moment that I realized that I was acting as my own attorney! Up until now, I thought that, the Assistant Attorney General, was my attorney. Instead, he was the attorney acting on behalf of the State of Michigan. I was indeed acting in pro-per, or in other words, representing myself. I suddenly felt small in the courtroom filled with chairs, the majority of them empty.

The Dominant Phone Provider's attorney asked for a brief recess, so he could talk to me in private. The recess was granted and we spoke together, without any witnesses. I was asked how much money would be sufficient to get me to back down—possibly $5,000? (Their legal department never approved this amount, and one would doubt the validity of such a claim anyway. He was just trying to get a feel for where we were at.) I bluntly rejected the offer. Prior to this hearing, I did receive a letter from their legal office suggesting that I accept an amount of approximately $1695.00.

The attorney began to speak on a different level, a slightly more personal tone. More like a stranger whom you engaged in conversation with, out of boredom, while waiting in line somewhere. I'm not sure if he was trying to play on my feelings or what. Maybe he thought that I was a pushover, but he said that he could lose his job if he lost this case. I'll admit, I did feel a little bad. The statement bounced around in my head, that afternoon. I didn't want anyone to lose their job or anything like that. I wasn't out to hurt anyone, only help them.

If only they would agree to change their current policies and verify new accounts immediately, to stop the fraud before it hit their front door. What ever happened to the days when you had to drive to the closest office, show a picture identification along with other personal information needed to obtain service? Did the greed for money and the demands to become the number one provider take over the importance of identity verification? Yes. No longer was accurate customer service the main objective...the almighty dollar won the battle.

I continued to ponder on what that attorney had said. Why should I feel sorry for him? Did anyone from his corporation demonstrate even a slight concern? Don't misunderstand me, after I filed the formal complaint, they cared. I began to receive phone calls from a now more urgent service provider. I received the respect that one deserved in the beginning. That's what running a business was all about. Taking care of the consumer should always remain number one, or the likelihood of failure is almost inevitable. It doesn't take a genius to figure that one out.

A monetary settlement along with a **promise** backed with a court order stating that they agreed to change their ways *would* have settled the whole thing.

I made a quick stop at the women's restroom and glanced in the mirror at the image of a woman who was not certain what her future held. Could I actually make a difference for the lives of other people? Was I wasting my own time, expending all of my own energy and possibly fighting a losing battle? I asked myself, "What in the world are you doing? Don't you know you're out of your league?"

I pulled out a tube of pink lip-gloss from my purse, applied it, and then took a second glance at my image reflecting back at me. I guess I *sort of* looked like an attorney ...when suddenly I felt a burst of confidence! I am right and they are wrong! I WILL NOT BACK DOWN!

I confronted the, soon- to- be jobless attorney and said, "If you are really that worried about losing your job, maybe you should ask for help or ask to be reassigned. Or, I suppose you could start looking for new employment!"

The court was adjourned for that day, due to an amended complaint that I filed. I found another rule that had been broken. The DPP needed more time. I would not return again for approximately a month. Great, more time to worry...or gain needed confidence!

Chapter 11

My Day to Be Heard!

Ironically enough, another storm hit our area the night before the hearing. I watched the local news and thought it was coincidental that Mother Nature was, somehow involved again. Luckily, this time, she wasn't that easily persuaded, there were no tornado's predicted. And I wasn't as nervous as I prepared myself for battle. Once again I had to pursue the roll of an attorney, fighting with all of my might to change the injustice.

Many people were warning me that I spoke too fast and this would not be good to do while on the witness stand. The judge would get aggravated if he couldn't understand me. Well, I came this far and I wasn't going to screw it up. I was once forced to speak more clearly when I held a position as a telemarketing agent for an office supply company. Even though it felt like slow motion to me, I knew I could do it.

A few times, I'll admit, I was stumped. I didn't have to worry how fast I was talking because I wasn't sure how to answer the question! I found it was better to take my time—and I caught myself staring into the microphone, which was placed six inches from my mouth. What seemed like an hour of indecisiveness was actually only minutes. I guess I was nervous after all and my knees were knocking under the podium.

My blue suit was left hanging in my closet. I couldn't make my second appearance in the same outfit. Instead, I wore a light brown, sleeveless, pantsuit. The courtroom was air conditioned, so I wore a white silk blouse under the vest, to avoid the Goosebumps. My tanned arms would have looked nice, but not professional. Besides, I had to look proficient. I wore laced brown shoes with a slight heel.

Once inside the courtroom, the introductions began, like before. Once again, Ron was sitting in the back of the room, on a chair against the wall. My new friend should have been sitting up front with the rest of us. Instead, this person, whose knowledge was quite amazing, was somehow left out of the situation. Thank goodness that the others were at my side. Every now and then they'd smile at me since it was obvious that I felt uneasy.

I was the first to be called to the witness stand. I began to walk up the steps leading to the microphone, when I was abruptly stopped. The DPP's attorney objected to the folder that I had in my hand. The Commission's attorney asked the judge to grant some slack, since I was a complainant acting on her own behalf.

The judge asked me if the papers in my hand were just notes. If so, could everyone have a copy of them? I opened my folder, gave them to the judge who then ordered duplicates to be passed out. Without my guidelines to follow, I would not have made a bit of sense.

Luckily, I was able to use them and I took my seat on the witness stand.

I was sworn in the traditional way —"Hold up your right hand and do you swear to tell the whole truth, nothing but the truth, so help you God?" I replied, "I do!" Then, for the record, I clearly stated my name along with spelling. I continued to say that I was acting in "Pro-Per." (It was beginning to feel like regular slang.) I had begun to assume the roll of the first accredited witness/ complainant.

The questions began, and a few times, I had to remind myself that I was talking too fast. (If everyone could talk as fast as I could, we'd be out of court in no time at all!)

The DPP's attorney began their line of questioning. He *tried* to divert the attention off of the DPP and onto the other creditors who happened to be on the same credit report. Two grocery stores and a gas station were amongst the list of fraudulent activity. (For amounts around one hundred dollars.) I treated them as I did the other dozen, years back. This time, I used certified mail.

The diversion failed when I made it clear that I had <u>no problem </u>in getting in touch with *their* credit departments. The others began the process of removing the derogatory information as soon as I notified them of the error. I had proven, to the both of them, that the accounts were fraudulent and I faced no argument. But still, the DPP's attorney continued as though the line of questioning was making a point—talking about others, instead of the problem at hand.

The strange thing about testifying as a witness was that they seemed to ask the same question, three or four times, hoping to get a different answer. The DPP began to dig deep into the Telecommunication Act and asked me to name which rules had been violated.

Unfortunately, I did not have this information with me. It was outlined in my attaché case, which was sitting on the floor, next to the chair I was at, before I was sworn in. I asked permission to leave the microphone to obtain the facts. Permission was granted, without a debate. I pushed my chair back away from the microphone. Carefully, I stepped down from the witness stand, praying that I wouldn't trip and fall flat on my face.

The DPP's attorney didn't seem to approve. I knelt down in front of my attaché case and began frantically thumbing through the papers. My hands were trembling from fear that I would fail to locate the information in time. Soon, the judge would call me back to the witness stand. *Secretly, in my head, I begged for help.* I had to find this one particular document, amongst hundreds of others, very quickly. Just when I began to feel the tension in the air, I found it! I proudly stood up and returned to my seat at the witness stand.

I feel that the defendant's attorney was trying to show that I was not acting on my own knowledge, but instead had been 'directed' by the public service commission. This is completely untrue. (This last statement cannot be made clear enough.) I did learn a lot from the state, but I was acting purely on my own desire.

The line of questioning resumed and I answered them, with the help of the newly retrieved paperwork. Suddenly, the DPP's attorney sneezed! Without thinking, I said, into the microphone, an audible *'God Bless you'*!

There was a moment of silence and the court stenographer recorded my words, then the line of questioning continued. (Now, when looking over the court transcripts, out of the blue, 'God Bless you' appears... without mentioning the sneeze that prompted the blessing. Not even a thank you was said either!)

It seemed like the DPP's attorney drilled me for quite some time. I'm sure he was hoping I would screw up, but I hadn't. I did a good job. My stomach had been performing summersaults but only I knew that.

Next, the Dominant Phone Provider called their first witness. She was asked questions on the procedures that they had in effect, back when my fraud began. She testified that safe guards *were* in use, back then and were currently used today, in the prevention of fraud.

What I still find extremely strange is this...the DPP came into court with very little documentation, I mean, nothing substantial. How could this be? They had to have paperwork somewhere, didn't they? Something had to be sent to the collection agency! <u>I think this made them look very bad</u>.

I, on the other hand, had kept an excellent paper trail, going back to 1996. I had enough letters and documents to fill a few archive file boxes! I kept waiting for *their* proof, but it **never** came.

Soon, the coffee that I consumed earlier had made its way to my full bladder. I thought my eyeballs were going to float out of my head. I crossed my legs hoping to relieve the pressure. I waited for the first witness to finish her testimony. Now, maybe we would get a small recess.

I was wrong; the next the DPP's witness was called up and sworn in. How in the world was I going to sit through another testimony? I grabbed a piece of paper and wrote Esther a note that read… "I don't suppose I can go to the restroom…I can't get up, can I?" Esther read my small message that I quickly scribbled down and then looked up at me and shook her head 'no.' Wonderful. Why didn't I leave the coffee in the pot this morning?

A dispute began over a letter. A letter that I swore, while under oath, that I never received. The DPP kept bringing the document up. I mumbled, what I thought to be quietly to myself, that I had never witnessed the document before.

Well, others heard my mumbling—one being the judge. Suddenly, he looked up and firmly scolded me, "Enough! I've heard enough!" I felt like a little kid who had just gotten in trouble. A little kid who had to go to the restroom, very, very badly. I suddenly couldn't wait for this thing to be over.

The next witness explained their procedures on verifying new accounts. They obtain a name and a social security number. The information is typed in to their system, which cross-references it to the credit agency. If the name and social security numbers match, then the account is opened. If the information failed to match, then further identification would be requested.

Well, this answered one of my questions…they **did not** have a policy which protected the public from fraud. Obviously, if someone had stolen a social security number, they're going to have the name too. Just by having a name and social security number, and without verifying the identification by picture I.D.—appeared to be utterly stupid to me. So, basically you could be whoever you wanted to be. Just get the information and you're on your way to a new identity. Did you want to be a doctor, a lawyer, or an airplane pilot? Just steal their info, and you're on your way. This <u>could</u> happen to anyone, after all!

How I hoped justice would prevail. How I hoped the judge would see how hard I had tried. Maybe, just maybe, he'd rule in my favor. Finally, court was adjourned for the day and I made the mad dash to the nearest ladies room!

Chapter 12

How Do I Write a Brief?

The court transcripts were delivered by Federal Express a few weeks later. Strangely enough, my DPP's phone service went 'out' the same day that the transcript arrived. Purely coincidental, I'm almost sure.

I'd be folding clothes and I'd hear a knock, knock, knock on the door. When I arrived to answer it, no one would be there. I'd look down on the first step and there lay a large envelope. It gave me a sort-of creepy feeling...could it be a mini bomb? (I have a vivid imagination! Maybe I should consider writing fiction next.)

I knew, after the transcripts arrived, I would have to get busy. Very busy, for I had no clue how to prepare a brief. (Basically, you review the transcripts and point out any areas that you agree or disagree with. Referring back to the transcript with a page number named within parentheses).

Writing the brief turned out to be a venting experience. It allowed me to express some of the feelings that I had been harboring, in the back of my mind. The blatant negligence demonstrated by the DPP's customer service department was the first to target. At last I had an outlet.

I worked, what seemed like, continually on this document. I wanted it to look as good as every other brief the commissioners would be viewing. I played around with the fonts on my computer until mine looked okay. (Although, I wish I had used a 12 sized font instead of an 11.) It appeared rather small, but other than that, I was impressed. The paper looked quite acceptable.

I mailed out copies to all concerned parties. The judge was very specific when he explained the rules to me. He focused his complete attention on me for a minute or so, explaining the court's intent. He continued on with explicit instructions on what was required of me. At this point, he stated that he didn't expect me to write a brief. But if I chose to do so, it was fine. It was to be mailed, in time, to meet the deadline. If I chose to abstain from writing one, he made it **very** clear that I was to write a letter informing him of my decision. He didn't want to be waiting for my paperwork to come straggling in. Although, he didn't have to wait since mine was the first brief to arrive in Lansing.

I heard the familiar knock, knock, knock and once again no one would be at the door, only another large envelope on the step below my feet. The DPP's brief was the first document to arrive at my home. The Commission's came the following day, probably due to the distance of the two in correlation to my residence. Mail traveling from Lansing may take a little longer compared to paperwork coming from Detroit.

I read the DPP's brief and I immediately began to sweat and my stomach turned over. After flipping through the pages of legal lingo, I began to feel that I was going to lose. I was up against a large corporation. BUT, this *very* large corporation was VERY wrong!

Then the next day, I'd receive the public service commission's brief —and I'd regain my confidence. Thus, the emotional roller coaster ride continued. The Commission definitely knew what they were doing. Their brief sounded phenomenal and believe me, I read it over and over, paying close attention to the wording.

Dennis and I were still without phone service; the landline coming into our home was not in use. Luckily, I had a competitors cellular phone that **was** functioning. The strange thing about this was why did everyone else on our street have a serviceable phone?

Mine remained out for about four days until I finally got a hold of Esther. She was able to make a call and amazingly enough had it was back in order the same day. (I should have called her sooner but I didn't think of it right away.)

I had only a week or so to prepare my reply brief. This time the task was handled with little or no help. I felt like had taken a crash course—and had retained quite a bit of knowledge. I wrote the entire document, then asked a few people to 'proof' it for me.

After the replies were all made, the judge would take his turn to ponder the paperwork and then make his recommendation. After careful deliberation he would then announce his opinion. If we disagreed with the opinion that the judge arrived at, then the weight fell on the three commissioners. The commissioners would each study the case and arrive at their own conclusion. Two of the three would have to concur on the decision.

It didn't take long for the ALJ, (Administrative Law judge), to arrive at his judgment. (Time flew by, for some reason. Maybe because I was busy working on the pool and with gardening.) He felt the DPP should be fined $40,000.00 **and** also change their current policies.

The question arose, "Do we accept the $40,000 and have the rules changed? Or do we put the commissioners to work?" I personally felt the suggested fine wasn't good enough. Believe it or not, the imposed fine could have been THIRTY MILLION! WOW....(was I ever glad that I kept that paper trail!)

It was determined that it _was_ necessary to involve the three commissioners. The ALJ's judgement and all of the documents would be passed on. It was now their turn to look over the paperwork and give their opinion. This would then become the final verdict, that is, unless an appeal was requested.

Chapter 13

Waiting 'Patiently'

Now that all of the legal paperwork was complete and I had done all that I could do, I tried to enjoy the summer. Not a day went by that I didn't think about the outcome. I only hoped that the time spent would benefit our system in some way.

The summer of 2000 was a strange season. The month of May was unseasonably hot and the kids and I bugged Dennis for a swimming pool. Then, after the pool was installed, June and July were unseasonably cool, with temperatures barely reaching the upper seventies. Needless to say, the pool was a pain in the rear, because whether we used it or not, it had to be maintained.

The Commissioners were on my mind. What decision will they arrive at? The possibility of them agreeing with the current ruling was realistic. As long as they ordered the rules to be changed, then the monetary part would be okay with me, although a higher fine was wished for. However, they were free to arrive at their own decision. I heard that it wasn't common for the commissioners to lower a proposed fine. They would either leave it as such, or possibly raise it. The power was in their hands. Hopefully, (and prayerfully), after careful examination, the fine would become significantly higher.

For some reason, I wanted my *story* to be heard. Maybe someday it would be known on a higher scale; and only time will reveal that answer. I knew others were faced with the same scenario. If I could attract the public's attention, I'd have a better chance in making a difference.

A hearing was scheduled in Washington D.C., on identity theft. How I wanted to serve as a panelist, or <u>just</u> be present at the hearing. My heart was so far into it, I felt, for sure, I could add something to this meeting. If only someone would have paid for the transportation, I would have gone in a heartbeat. I even had a sitter lined up for K.J.

Unfortunately, the airfare was too high. (Over Six Hundred dollars.) I was' bummed out' when it didn't materialize. Dennis wasn't disappointed in the least and was relieved when my plans fell through. He didn't like the idea of his wife traveling to Washington, alone. He and his brother John would be in Nova Scotia on a hunting trip.

My nerves were getting to me, since I knew 'D-day' was close at hand. I wasn't feeling very well. Then, the long awaited call came, late one Friday afternoon. The answering machine was taking the calls and Esther phoned to inform me that the hearing was indeed scheduled. You could tell that Esther was anxious and wondered about the verdict. She had put forth a tremendous amount of effort and her heart was in this thing as much as mine was.

It was not required that I attend the scheduled meeting. Esther knew it was a two-hour drive but I asked her to inform me of the date. I knew I might never have a closure to the situation if I didn't see it all of the way through.

My stomach was feeling sort of queasy and I wasn't sure if I could make it to Lansing. It was only going to be a five-minute meeting and surely someone could give me the answer, over the phone. (I **must** have been feeling poorly! I can't imagine the thought of not seeing this thing through until the very end! After I had just spend all of that time and energy and I wasn't going to hear the final conclusion?)

The night before, I ironed my clothes, just in case I decided to make the two—hour drive. Of course, sleep was scarce that night and I found myself wide-awake at Four a.m. As I lay there in bed, I pondered the trip in my head. When, all of the sudden, I heard a beeping coming from the living room area. I got up and followed the faint sound. It wasn't coming from the living room, after all, so I continued on into the kitchen. I opened the silverware drawer and ironically enough, a travel alarm clock was going off! (We had taken the small clock with us on our trip to Key West, some five months earlier. For some reason, while unpacking the motor home, I stuck it in the kitchen drawer.)

Well, that made up my mind. Hmmm, maybe God wanted me go. Or perhaps I would strongly regret it, if I hadn't made the effort. I began to get ready, only this time, I basically slapped on a little make up, combed my hair, and quickly dressed. I wasn't making a major appearance, so what the heck.

I quietly slipped out of the house at six o'clock and headed to the nearest gas station for a fill up and a weak cup of coffee. (My stomach just couldn't handle too much Java.) Would I win or lose? Would I cry if I lost? Yes, of course I would. I cry very easily, which is not a good trait. I'd prefer to cry in the privacy of my own home though.

Chapter 14

"Yahoo!"

The drive to Lansing was starting to feel quite routine. It resembled a drive into work and I actually didn't mind the traveling, all that much. (I'm sure if it became a daily journey; I would grow tired of it.)

I'd pop in a C.D. and sing the whole way there. I *was* rather nervous this time. Perhaps more uptight than when I was driving into Lansing to testify. Today, it would be over and if the verdict did not go my way, I would have to face it like a woman…and a good sport. (A good sport, me? Not when it comes to ***outright injustice***.)

I stopped at the rest area located close to the Commission's office, since my bladder was going to burst! I then called my sister, Laurie, from my cell phone. She was surprised that I had decided to go, since the night before I had a pretty good migraine going. The back of my neck ached terribly. It was so intense I began to wonder about the recent Meningitis outbreak. (A friend from high school just lost his life to the disease.

We weren't close, but he was an acquaintance and I felt bad.)

Laurie asked if I was nervous and if I still had the awful headache and I answered her with, "My head is a little better but I'm petrified!" She wished me a quick "good luck" and I was on my way.

Ron saw me as I walked up to the building to the entrance located outside his office. He opened the door and acted surprised to see me. Esther met me with a big smile and I followed her to her work cubicle. I could tell that she and Ron were both pleased that I came. We all worked together so well over the past months. In ten minutes we'd be entering the courtroom. Esther inquired if Justine knew that 'today was the day'. I hadn't called her; so it appeared that Justine had no clue that the verdict would soon be announced.

I asked Esther if the press would cover the story and she said that it all depended on the verdict. Sometimes things don't get publicity and she was not certain. It all depended on the final outcome.

The courtroom would be called to order, only for a brief five minutes or so, purely to announce the verdict. Then, the following day, the whole thing would be over. I thought to myself, "I'll have to get a job after all of this...what in the world will I do with all of my time?"

Esther and I took a seat in the courtroom that already had a few people waiting. One person was from the DPP, but I don't know which one they were. Whoever they were certainly kept quiet.

The woman in front of me held papers in her hands. I didn't mean to be nosey, but I could read the bold title,

"Press Release." My heart jumped in my chest! It appeared that there was going to be a press release after all! I wanted people to know and hoped they would follow where I lead.

The three commissioners entered the courtroom and didn't waste any time. The room was called to order. Each made their introduction then continued on with the news we had been waiting for.

I held my breath when one started to speak. The words that I am quoting are not the exact language used, but they went something like this, "Case number 12336, Nelski vs. the DPP," one of the commissioners began. He continued, "We find the DPP guilty. The fine imposed is one and a half million dollars."

I was expecting a much smaller fine and when I heard the verdict I let out an audible 'squeal' of joy! Esther sort of elbowed me, since I was the only one who made a peep. I was overjoyed so instead of saying anything else, I clutched my hands into fists and shook them up and down. I couldn't believe my ears…one and a half million dollars? I was elated with the news. I did it! I WON! HA, HA, HA…and it had been said, more than once, that I couldn't do it! The next three minutes seemed like forever while they continued to explain how they derived at the fine.

We walked out into the hall and I was congratulated on my 'job well done.' The woman who sat kiddy corner in front of me came up, introduced herself, and shook my hand. She was the press consultant who earlier held the papers in her hand. She gave me a few copies of the release.

I thanked her for the documents and told her that I had to make a few more copies of it. Then I was heading home to make some phone calls. She handed me two more copies then said, "Honey, this is going on the wire in a moment or two."

I obviously didn't know what 'going on the wire' meant. I replied, "That's good! Well thank you, everyone, for your help." I turned to Esther and gave her a quick hug. I had grown to care about her. She was now a friend of mine. Who knows maybe a friend for life? You just can't forget about people who have contributed so much of their time and obviously had genuine feelings. I told Esther that I'd keep in touch with her and call every now and then, just to 'bug' her!

I went to the restroom before starting my drive back to Carleton. I washed my hands and looked in the mirror. I smiled the biggest smile back at myself. I was rather pale and didn't look normal, but I had a grin that was from *ear to ear*! Boy was I glad that I decided to come! Thank goodness for that travel alarm clock that mysteriously went off in the kitchen. (It has never gone off on its own before.)

I walked outside, into the chilly air, and pulled my coat up around my neck. I made it to my car and I opened the door, put the papers on the passenger seat and immediately called Dennis from my cell phone. He was proud of me and said that I 'knocked sparks in their ass.'

He wanted to know when I'd be home and I told him that I was going shopping on the way home to pick up a few groceries. I said I'd be back in about three hours. I quickly called Shirley, and my sister Laurie. After those calls, I also dialed my mom. I was so pleased with myself, I just had to call and spread the good news! I even tried calling Dr. Go but he was not at work!

Chapter 15

My Fifteen Minutes of Fame!

I took my good ol' sweet time in Meijers and even began my Christmas shopping. It was early to start since it was only September, but I was in a great mood and couldn't help myself. *I was so happy* and I wondered if my joy was visible to others around me. I wanted to tell everyone that I bumped into about the verdict, but I would have looked like I was crazy. I kept my mouth shut instead.

By the time that I pulled into our driveway, Dennis met me at my car. Before I even opened the door, he motioned for me to roll down the window. It was apparent he had something very important to tell me. He was acting a little strange, I mean, I'd be out of the car in a second or two anyway. He had the phone up to his ear.

I rolled down the window and he said, "Get out of the car, I'll bring all of the bags in! Channel Four will be here in ten minutes! They're just around the corner! The phone hasn't stopped ringing! Don't you want to change or something? The camera crew is with them. Channel 50 is on their way too! The rest will be following!"

The excitement my husband showed hyped me up immediately. He said that he couldn't get a thing done, for the phone kept ringing and ringing and ringing! He was right; I did want to change. I was going to be all over the news and I hadn't even showered yet that day! And remember, I just 'slapped on my make-up that morning'…

Once in the house, I let out another squeal of joy and quickly picked up my dog, Mariah, and hugged her. She's a little black and white Shih Tzu-Poodle and is as sweet as can be. I held her in my arms and twirled around in the living room. But, I knew I had to hurry, so I put her in her bed and ran into my bedroom. I slipped on a pair of Levi's and a black and white v-neck sweater.

I looked in the mirror at my hair and how I wished I had showered that morning! I quickly touched up my make up when before I knew it, Dennis was calling me into the living room. The first interview was about to take place.

I turned on the blow dryer and fluffed up my hair a little. They would have to wait another minute or two. I was so excited! It felt like I was in the middle of a dream or something!

During the interview with Channel Four, the phone continued to ring. The Associated Press requested an interview, so Dennis took down their phone number. WJR requested a live radio interview and ended up playing the blurp every fifteen minutes.

Luckily, I was able to take a quick shower before the next 'appointment' arrived. I felt a lot better after getting cleaned up and continued on with the interviews. ABC,

NBC, CBS, and Fox all showed up that day. The story even made National television and CNN picked it up too. CNN didn't say my name but described me as 'a Michigan woman'. The Public Service Commission was getting calls from the East Coast!

By Five O'clock, I was ready to sit down and relax. The adrenaline rush that I experienced during day left me feeling drained. The phone was still ringing though. My friend Dominic heard me on WJR and called to congratulate me. Nancy, Kelli and Diane, a few other friends of mine, called after seeing me on TV. Ricky, a work associate of Dennis, called to say that he and his wife were happy for my achievement.

The next day, I ran a few errands and was recognized. "Miss, are you the one who was on television last night?"

I looked up to discover that people were staring at me. I simply answered, "Yes-that was I."

The woman who asked the question replied with, "Thanks!" Now, that was cool, she said 'thanks' to me! I'll admit, I liked the attention. My picture was on the cover of quite a few newspapers. That's probably why people were spotting me.

Somehow, it didn't feel like it was 'over'. I don't know why I felt this way, but could it be over, just like that? I had a feeling that the DPP would appeal, so how could it be completely over?

Chapter 16

You Messed With the Wrong Redhead!

I hadn't realized the magnitude of what I had done and perhaps still don't. In fact, after talking to Lenny, an attorney friend of mine, I hung up the phone in a state of wonder. He said, "You don't realize this now, but you may have changed the future dramatically. You are the new Erin Brockovich, not the out dated one!"

It was funny to hear him mention Erin Brockovich, because, not a month earlier, Dr. Go told me to go see the movie. He said that I would relate to her story and perhaps it would provide me with inspiration. Dr. Go wrote down Erin's name and 'ordered' me to watch it. I went to the video store immediately after exiting his office, but the movie hadn't been released on video yet. So then, I tried to see it at the movie theater, but it had already been removed from the viewing list. I had no choice but to wait, in limbo, until I could finally see it for myself. And he was right; Julia Roberts did an excellent performance, as usual.

Somehow, I did not feel that my task was quite the same as Erin's. Going up against a huge corporation, now, in this instance the scenario was the same. But the nature of her case was completely different.

Erin dug up information, on her own time, and helped families whom had lost a family member, or a member who was suffering with serious, irreversible health challenges in their lives. She was able to organize and win a class action lawsuit by suing for punitive damages caused from the Chromium that was dumped into a nearby stream. The Chromium entered the underground water supply that was used to drink, wash, and for everything that water was used for.

I am simply someone who fought for her rights. I had the hopes of stopping this identity theft problem, **dead** in its tracks. If I could prevent this from happening to just one person—then my journey would have been worth it. This was my goal throughout the years of battle and **is** what kept my engines running.

At times my goal did become hazy. Hearing negativity and allowing it to sink in your brain can cause you to fail. I've heard, "You'll never win, do you think the verdict will be in your favor? No way...you're dealing with the DPP." The negativity would be rejected from my ears...and I would respond with, "You're wrong! I am going to win this thing. I just *have* too!"

Sad, but true, the negative statement could have become a reality. I was dealing with the DPP who had attorneys employed that were making *thousands of dollars a day.* (Someone estimated it, somewhere along the line...)

The truth here is, I didn't know if I could handle it if I would have lost. I may have ended up with a severe case of depression, or something. I had allowed the circumstance to completely consume me. Don't ask me where the energy came from. (Oh yea, I knew from where…God. I knew he was on my side, because I talked to him daily.)

I was definitely treading on new ground. At times, things did get hairy. In one of the documents, the DPP made a few comments that, I'll admit, got under my skin. They slammed me pretty good! One of the statements went something like this—once again –this is not an exact quote, "they did not wish to continue to have dealings with a complainant acting as her own attorney; but they had no choice but to defend themselves vigorously…." My interpretation of that statement is this; 'she can't afford an attorney—so why bother with her?'

Affording an attorney wasn't the case at all, but rather, 'finding an attorney.' I couldn't even find one to discuss the issue with. It felt as if the DPP were rubbing it in my face that I had no prior legal experience. If I was meant to win, I'll win and *you* can't stop me!

When I read the insult, it made me angry. But in a round about way, it may have done some good. The statement simply made me more determined. It added *more fuel to my fire*, so to speak. This was good because at times I thought my fuel would run out.

I was relieved that the verdict was announced and the testimony was over. However, the phone was still ringing. Somehow, people were getting my phone number. On a few occasions, people would call one of the television stations for my information and ask permission to call me. It was apparent that others wanted to talk about their own horror story involving the DPP. A few people actually inquired if they could come over for me to review their paperwork. I explained that I was also treading on unstable ground. What could I do to help all of these people? For the moment, all I could do was listen. Besides that, I didn't need strangers coming over.

I was **so** thankful for the victory! Perhaps there was a greater power at work. Perhaps the entire scenario was preplanned. God guided me to the path and led me. Maybe I was meant to go through the whole ordeal. It had affected me so deeply...

Chapter 17

You Go Girl!

How funny, the phone just rang and it was the DPP. (When the caller identified herself, my heart jumped.) The woman called to offer me a voice pager, on a free trial basis. And for just trying it, I would receive a check for $16! I chuckled, out loud and the lady on the other end was not sure if I was crazy or what....

I asked her what state she was calling from? Was she from Michigan and did she know about the 1.5 Million dollar fine? Was this a joke or what? Well, she wasn't from Michigan and hadn't heard a thing about the recent fine.

I apologized to her for my behavior, since <u>I'm sure</u> I sounded sarcastic. She then informed me that she didn't work for the DPP, but a firm hired purely for promotional services only. When she hung up, she was laughing and told me to have a wonderful, wonderful day!

After hanging up the phone, I glanced up at the clock and noticed that it was time to pick up my stepdaughter, Amanda. She and Melissa live with their mother and stepfather a few miles away. A few days a week the kids come over to eat dinner and to hangout with K.J. I quickly drove to pick Amanda up then headed straight back home. As I pulled the car back up to our driveway, I noticed that the mail had arrived.

I opened the mailbox and there was a box stuffed inside. I thought it was something for Dennis since he's always getting parts delivered. He's constantly working on some kind of machinery—cars, boats, RV's, you name it.

Giving gifts has always been a rewarding experience for me; however, I find it hard to accept them. But, receiving one, through the mail is rather hard to refuse. I put my hand into the mailbox and grabbed the package, but had a hard time removing it since it was packed in pretty good. I removed the carton and was surprised to see my name on the label. I smiled and couldn't imagine who would send me a gift...maybe it was a late birthday present?

I handed it to Amanda, so she could open it for me, while I continued down the long driveway that led to our house. She started to open the box when she suddenly changed her mind. She said, "No Pat, it's **your** gift...**you** open it!"

We went in the house and sat on the kitchen floor and began to open the surprise present. (We *really* do have chairs in our house! It seems like every story involves sitting on the floor, which is the worst thing for my back. Maybe the sitting, cross-legged, position stems from my Native American heritage——?)

The package was from my sister and brother -in-law, Sheryl and John. I opened the card first. (I don't like it when people skip right over the card and head straight for the gift.) I smiled when I saw the cover of it. It was a cartoon girl showing off her muscles with large words that read, "YOU GO GIRL!" I continued to read the card, enjoying the congratulations it relayed. Others were appreciative of my efforts and this, in itself, was rewarding and made the recent achievement all worth the while.

The box was filled with bubble wrap, the kind that people cannot resist on popping. So, needless to say, Amanda and I destroyed a few before continuing. Inside the bubble wrap hid the movie, "Erin Brockovich!" I laughed, *again*, and immediately picked up the phone to call and thank them.

Sheryl said that her boss read about the report on the Internet and wanted to know if she and I were related. She 'admitted' that we were indeed related and spoke about buying me the movie. (Sheryl is one of my kind of people...**always** giving.) They spoke about the case for awhile and figured that I probably had five copies of the movie already! Well, I didn't have my own copy, but had viewed it, twice. There's no doubt I would have made the purchase, somewhere down the line. I had it in my hands, a few times already, then changed my mind. Besides, this gift meant more to me.

I felt that Erin's battle was different, although parts of it were similar. The helplessness that she felt at times, her drive and determination that kept her going. Now, those traits remind me of myself. In the movie, she's firm on getting to the bottom of the situation and lost many nights of sleep worrying, I'm sure. But in the end, justice prevailed and her efforts made a difference for many people. Erin had to feel wonderfully proud to be an American and that her helping hand —*helped*!

Chapter 18

Is A Civil Suit the Next Step?

My fifteen minutes of fame was definitely over. I wasn't being noticed in the grocery store or the local pizza shop any longer! I didn't expect it to continue long, but it was fun while it lasted.

I was still giving advice to people when they happened to get in touch with me. I could remember what it was like when no one seemed to care and did not know what advice to offer. It was as if the DPP had become such a giant, they were untouchable. They could afford the legal fees, where as a small firm could drown if all of their time was spent doing research. (Research, involving law issues takes a lot of time and a small firm could suffer.) If defeated, this could ruin their business completely, like the movie we've been comparing.

I, on the other hand, had time. Lucky, for me, I was between jobs and was able to prepare my own legal documents. I was faced with uncertainty, just the way a law firm would be unsure of the pending verdict. In my heart, I felt as if I would win. *It wasn't fair* the way this corporate giant was allowed to conduct business. They should be punished for the stress that they have caused **along** with being fined.

I was considering a class action suit...but I needed to take a break first. Time to think about my next move. A visit to the library became an objective. The reaction that confronted me was one that urged to me to continue. (Even though I didn't feel ready to go on.) When the topic of identity theft arose, I found out that many others were feeling defeated too.

Perhaps, someday, I'll be able to make a difference. Possibly the laws will be looked at and new ones thought up with the intention of preventing future fraud. Even though my 'fame' was now over, I felt that good was accomplished.

My health had come a long way too. I often spoke to Dr. Go about the DPP. I expressed my new concerns and the possible pending legal action. He looked at my chart and decided that it was time for some routine blood work. I would have to be healthy to undergo another battle. This one would require more effort— I think.

When I signed in at the lab, I was surprised to see numerous patients waiting to have their blood drawn. The lab had just moved down the hall and it was clear that they were still trying to get adjusted to their new location. I was informed that the current wait time was about an hour. Well, I had no desire to sit in a waiting room filled with dozens of sick people, so I asked if it would be okay if I signed in. Then I could run a few errands and return in a little while. The receptionist said that that would be fine.

After going by the bank and my parent's home, I returned. I noticed that the parking lot seemed a little less full and I began my brisk walk to the rotating door. I began pushing the door, vigorously, since they're rather heavy and force is required to make them move. The next thing I remembered was hearing someone scream, "Hey...STOP...Hey!"

I looked up and I saw a little old lady, directly across from me, in her pie shaped walking area of the revolving door. The frail woman was not seen earlier since she was rather small and very hunched over. Her entire silhouette was hid perfectly behind the divider in the door.

She looked up and appeared to be really mad at me! I stopped walking as soon as I realized she was in the door too...but she still looked hateful! I felt just awful! Here I was, feeling pretty good and full of energy and here she was barely walking.

I met her outside and I began to apologize, "I'm *so* sorry! I'd never want to hurt you!" I gently touched her on the shoulder and asked her if she was okay. I mean, what a better place to get hurt at, than a hospital. I could take her right back in, if she needed to go.

I think her daughter was with her and I looked up and said, "Are you sure she's fine? I didn't see her in the door! I'm really sorry!"

The daughter replied, "She's fine. She is more shaken up than anything else. There is a blind spot in the door."

Well, she didn't look fine to me. She was using a four-legged walking cane and I thought she was going to wop me over the head with it, at any moment. I can understand being a little upset, but I didn't see her plus the fact that I apologized over and over again.

Here I was, going faster than a rabbit and she was as slow as a turtle. I do not suggest someone that walks that slowly to go through a rotating door. The "handicapped' exit would be more preferable, don't you think?

This shows that my course of treatment was working and I was getting my old energy back. It might have been the release of the stress that I was under, since I won against the DPP. I was pleased that I wasn't bullied down. And most of all, I was pleased that I didn't give up, but instead stood up for what I knew was wrong!

Chapter 19

"Dear Patty, Not Dear Abby!"

That's how it's been lately! "Dear Patty!" That's okay, you could say it was my turn to listen to others. Therefore, I was brushing up on listening skills instead of talking all of the time.

The people that I had spoken with, by either phone or the Internet, all seemed to be at their wits end. A few of them even broke down and cried! Almost as if they' were on the verge of a nervous breakdown with no where to turn. I've certainly had been there and I did not have the heart to ignore them.

And believe me, it is all started to play on my mind. They would like a class action lawsuit begun, with me the leader. I've been hearing, "Come on Patricia, we need you!" I told them that I would gladly compile a list of names for *them*, but that I didn't feel strong enough for another battle.

The family grew tired of the subject again. Can you blame them? Hearing chatter of the same subject day in and day out. It became apparent to me when one of them finally said, "Pat, enough is enough!"

But, I was still confused and I needed to talk! I had stopped therapy years earlier, but felt, once again, that I could use a second opinion. Counseling seemed to give me the courage to continue. My therapist, Carmen, agreed that I had every reason to feel confused. Knowing that the criminal was still running free never helped matters in the slightest.

I resumed therapy and it felt good to have professional advice close at hand. One day at a time became my motto. I was fighting for a cause. I had the documentation, so why not continue?

I'll have to admit the more victims that I listened to; the madder I became. These people were desperate. I imagine they sounded similar to how I did back then. Like life wasn't stressful enough with all of its ups and downs. Who needs to spend every spare moment fighting?

I found out that the Public Service Commission was holding a hearing, in a nearby city. A man who had viewed my story on TV sent an E-mail, informing me of the meeting. I decided to attend and get the feel for how many others were troubled. I threw on a pair of dress pants and a sweater, grabbed my attaché' case and headed for the meeting.

I was surprised to see how many cars were there. I had a hard time finding a parking spot so I parked on a side street and walked over. The media was there to get the latest scoop on the good old DPP.

Walking in, late as usual, during the introductions, I raised my hand in the air until it was my turn to introduce myself. I stood up and suddenly became nervous! I began to stutter, which is something that doesn't normally happen to me. Then finally, I regained my composure and said, "My name is Patty Nelski and I'm...the person, who took on the DPP...and won!"

After receiving a small standing ovation, I heard clapping and cheering. My face must have turned three shades of red. I actually felt the blood rush to my face and I thought one could see my heart beating just by watching my throat.

The public service hearing was called to order and quiet came over the room. I glanced around at the packed meeting. There were men and women of all ages. Some were dressed in suits while others simply in blue jeans. They were all there for basically the same reason...to express their grief about their phone service.

After hearing the first few complaints, it seemed apparent that most were in attendance because of all of the downed phone lines, not because of identity theft. Some households had been without phones for weeks on end. I was hoping to run into a few people whom had situations similar to mine. It had only been a week since my story hit the headline news announcing the 1.5 million-dollar verdict.

After listening to several speakers an elderly man approached the podium. I felt bad when he began to speak. His voice was frail and I could hear the quiver in his pronunciation and this touched me. Now, I KNOW he didn't need this in his life. I had to get up from my chair and exit the room; the story was that bothering to me.

Quietly, I exited the meeting and began looking for the woman's restroom when I heard, "Ms. Nelski! Please wait! Ms. Nelski!" Wow, someone was chasing down the hallway after me! I turned around, to face the shouting, and answered, "I'm not leaving, I am looking for the restroom."

After finishing up, I returned to the meeting and began taking notes. I was surprised how many people wanted to talk to me! Some of them didn't seem to care that it was another's turn at the microphone and continued right on with their own saga, ignoring the person who was already had the floor and was speaking.

I noticed two DPP representatives standing, to my right side, against the wall. I overheard one of them say, "There she is—and she's taking notes. It looks like she's writing down names." (I chuckled again as I thought to myself, "They're afraid of me...and I'm really not a bad person!")

I ended up speaking to a half a dozen people who were victims of fraud. I wrote down their names and phone numbers. One woman had twenty-two phones opened in her name! Imagine how frustrated she must have felt?

I asked one lady for her name and phone number then handed her my spiral notebook. Before I knew it, she had it for the rest of the time we were there! I kept saying, "Ma'am, I have to leave to pick up my son. Can I have my notebook back?"

She'd reply with, "I'm almost done!" I would wait another minute or so, then I'd ask again," Excuse me, but I have to pick up my son and he has homework to do!" The woman was so engrossed in what she was writing, it was as if she *couldn't* stop.

The meeting lasted past dark and I listened to many people that evening. I'm not sure if I helped any of them. Hopefully, just the act of lending an ear was a start in the right direction. I'm think I helped the lady with the spiral notebook, because her story alone filled up quite a few pages!

Chapter 20

An Apology? Not a Chance!

My friends in Lansing were assuring me that I *had* made a big difference. (Although I was not in the position to observe the changes and probably never will be.) Somehow, I hadn't felt like I had done enough.

Esther called to see if my phones were quieting down. She said that their 'thermometer' blew off of the chart. I guess they were keeping track of their progress, cases that were won—that sort of thing, by using a graph that had a thermometer on it. The 'temperature' went up with each case that was won. Well, the 1.5 Million—dollar fine that was won, for the State of Michigan, caused the thermometer to exceed its capacity!

So, in honor of the day that the verdict was announced, a luncheon day was scheduled, to celebrate the event. " The Patty Nelski Luncheon Day" sounded amusing, but also pretty thoughtful!

Needless to say, the DPP decided to appeal the verdict as predicted. I guess that's the way the 'law game' was played. I wouldn't be surprised if the whole thing was held up, in court, for years to come.

Too bad the DPP hadn't just paid the fine, without going through the entire appeal process. So, in the mean time, not only was the money being held up but also the new rules that I hoped for. And to me, the rules were the <u>most important</u> part!

This angered me, but I guess this was the normal law procedure. (Please do not forget, the fine for this offense could have been thirty million.) I think 1.5 was letting them off easy.

I was surprised that they didn't appeal **my** monetary portion too. They probably said, "Let's get this red-headed, pain in the butt out of our way!" The check came in the mail the following week.(And just for the record, the amount that I received was under $3,000.)

One thing *was* proven to me— I viewed the world in an unrealistic way. I don't know what I expected! Perhaps a tiny letter that simply said, "Sorry." Nothing came but a check that resembled a child support payment, with the snap off ends.

I thought in the end, I would have gained an ounce of respect from them. I've been laughed at, continually, for that wish…but it's true. That's just me, trying to see the good in all. They haven't tried to apologize, to me personally, but if they would have, I certainly would have called the media. (Well, I guess that statement isn't *completely* true. A spokesperson for the company did say they were "sympathetic towards the victim". I think that was said for the public viewpoint though.) Anyway, if they had tried, it would have appeared that there was a *heart* somewhere in the company. Their noble effort would have been a chance for a positive public statement, but they blew that one too.

That's poor customer service—isn't it? Well, that's par for the course. No customer service in the beginning so why would one expect anything other than that? Even a quick, little one-liner-letter *simply* stating the words "Sorry for the inconvenience." Or just, "Sorry" would have been sufficient.

"Wake Up Patty, this is the *real* world!" Ha! Say sorry? I had just cost them **a lot** of money and negative publicity and to think that I had been waiting for an apology letter? I needed to wake up and smell the roses, didn't I?

Why did I feel an urge to continue? I wasn't sure in what aspect yet, but I felt pulled, never the less. For whatever reason, it was on my mind continually. Was it because it wasn't meant to be over? *I didn't feel* as if it was over, almost as if it had just begun.

I was expecting a call from a man that lived in South Dakota. Now, what could he possibly want? And how did he hear about me in the first place? I wasn't sure if I could help someone that lived in South Dakota, could I? I grew curious and figured the call would come soon. I was definitely interested in what he had to say.

Chapter 21

The Billboard

Unless the DPP decides to review their policies, the fraud will continue on. It's almost like a sinking ship. If you have one hole in your vessel, water will leak in. Fraud will sneak in, if it's allowed to happen. Now, with the appeal process underway, I had to come to grips with the fact that 'we" might *still* lose. The majority of rulings lie against me. In other words, the corporations usually win and us 'little people' lose. I refused to give up and to allow negative thinking to be a part of this charade.

I had been trying to take it easy and secure the time to sort out my thoughts. Well, my thoughts weren't any neater than they were a week prior! I then asked God to show me a sign of some sort. How I wished he could just write me a darn letter with instructions—or pick up the phone and call me. Suddenly, the phone rang and on the other end was a man with a heavy southern accent. (Wow, God had a southern accent!) You know they're from the Deep South when they start out the conversation with, "Ma'am…" I thought this was the call that I had been expecting from South Dakota, too bad it couldn't have been God!

Apparently, he had heard the fifteen-second "blurp" on the radio while driving his car in Tallahassee, Florida. The caller was Mike Tomsley who had taken the time to call from his cell phone. He said, "It was sort of like a miracle...I've been working on this case for my client and the situation is alot like yours. May I ask, who is your attorney?"

When he found out that I didn't have one, he began to talk to me about pursuing the case, as a civil matter. He was very kind and I find it strange that he called me, from Florida. Before he hung up, he said he'd call again, as soon as he found a break through in his case. (Although, the complaint wasn't about the DPP, but another phone service provider.)

Then, the following night, the phone rang again and Amanda answered it then handed it to me. This time it was the man from South Dakota. This time, the call was not from an attorney looking for advice, but a victim of identity theft. He was just beginning his battle, but chose to handle his situation in court. He was in the process of filing a civil suit.

Then, while driving down the expressway I was deep in thought. Very deep...and when I concentrate with such intensity, my eyebrows furrow and unfortunately I have permanent 'thinking lines' on my forehead. My thoughts continued as I drove, "Should I continue, or should I drop it?" (Eeny, meeny, miney, MO—should I continue, or let it go? Oops...another dumb joke...)

My heart *felt* as if it was *trying to get through to me*, when all of the sudden I looked up at the advertisements along the highway and noticed a huge black billboard coming up quickly to my left side. In moments, it was in front of me and clearly visible. It said, "DON'T MAKE ME COME DOWN THERE!"...And it was signed, "**GOD!**"

I said, out loud in my car, "Okay, okay, I'll find an attorney *and* I'll write a book!" Immediately I felt rushes of energy go through my body—we'll call them the shivers, followed by the Goosebumps that covered me from head to toe!

After all of the prompting, I finally began making phone calls, in pursuit of an attorney who would represent me, on a contingent basis. Maybe this time someone would agree to talk to me. After all, I had the original court transcripts in my hand. I hoped that I'd be able to find an attorney to handle the case. (And not be 'chicken' to go up against the mammoth corporation, like the rest of them were, years earlier.)

What laws had been violated? I knew fraud, in itself, was illegal, but was it hard to enforce? I'd at least go and talk to someone to see if a class action was even a possibility. Who knows, the 'statue of limitations' may have expired. (The time limit one has to seek legal action.) I didn't know for sure if I was on the right path but I guess a few phone calls wouldn't hurt.

How does one know if they're doing the right thing? I tried to follow my heart but this became difficult at times. We knew that the DPP, and the other creditors for that matter, were all very negligent in handling my identity crisis. (The word 'negligent' is too gentle of a description.) They just didn't care nor had the time to deal with the problem. Perhaps it was plain and simply <u>too time</u> consuming!

Chapter 22

"This is a Test..."

Afriend of mine made a comment to me that went like this, "I can't wait to see what happens...when something happens to a 'little person', will she win in the court of law? Or will the big corporation win? You know, MONEY TALKS!"

Well, Heather wasn't the only one who was curious. Others around were asking the same question but there's no simple answer. Heather works at our family's dentist—orthodontist. I tell you, time flies by...I've been seeing Dr. Grasso and his staff for over twenty years now!

I was recently getting some dental work done and it was a unanimous agreement that I needed to 'chill out' for a few minutes. Soon, the rubber clown nose was placed on my face and I fell under the spell of the laughing gas. Then I began to think. It's hard to concentrate when you shut your eyes and you're consumed in a pink ocean of swirling dots. I didn't like that I couldn't concentrate so I opened my eyes and asked for a piece of paper and an ink pen. I was clearly fighting the gas, so I finally gave in and shut my eyes. They were right—I needed to 'chill out.'

The City of Detroit honored me with The Annual Consumer Award, in February of 2001. The certificate states, "In recognition of her extraordinary efforts to protect the rights of all Michigan consumers." The City Of Detroit's golden seal matches the gold colored mat that frames the certificate. If the presentation had been given a week later, I probably would have cried. (Maybe. PMS is unpredictable.)

This was the first time that I had ever met Justine face to face. Up until now we were just phone friends. She's a sweet person—only God knows how much assistance she was and how much I appreciated it. She came along, when I was at my wits end and needed a friend who knew what she was doing.

A few of the television networks were at the ceremony to cover the story. Since it was rather chilly outside, I layered up. First with a silky blue tank top, then a blue turtle neck sweater, and **then** my blue suit coat!

To top it off, I was fifteen minutes late! I was busy in the women's restroom, removing a layer of clothes. The turtleneck was overwhelming on the sixteenth floor of the Cadillac tower building. Heat rises and it was really warm. Luckily, I had that tank top on under all of those layers!

The one thing about the camera was, I sort-of let my guard down or something. Either that or I forget that cameras were rolling! I was asked the question, "What was your darkest hour?" Well, I had two bad ones, the initial discovery and when the DPP appeared four years later on my credit report. I stated the truth however, as corny as it sounded! I said, "When I found out the second time, I was devastated. I didn't think I could fight another battle...then I began to cry. I ended up on my kitchen floor, like a loony lady!" GREAT! Boy do I wish I could take that statement back! Then, another popular announcer asked me the title of my book and when I stated the name, I made this awful, goofy smile. I wish I could take back that smile too.

Another question that caught me off guard was," What makes you keep getting up to fight? Where do you get your stamina?" Well, I thought about for a moment and I almost got religious on them. But after all, I was only receiving an award so the answer had to be short. So, I replied with, "If you've ever known a Red-head, you'll know of their temper! Try putting a cap it!" Everyone began to laugh.

I liked the story prelude that was used this time on TV...not "David and Goliath" but "David **slays** Goliath!" Another smile popped on my face. And I was honored to be a biblical character!

After the award ceremony, the Director of Consumer Affairs, Mr. John Roy Castillo, treated me to an elegant lunch. Reservations had been made at the "Caucus", a little restaurant in the heart of Detroit, which was on the expensive side, I thought.

We walked there from the Cadillac Tower building. Thankfully, it was a mild day and not the extreme cold that we had been experiencing. It didn't take us long to arrive at the restaurant. We checked our coats soon after entering, although the thought crossed my mind to hang onto it, since I was always cold, except for on the sixteenth floor an hour earlier.

Luckily, it was rather cozy and warm and the overhead lights were turned down to a comfortable level. Guess what I ordered? (No, not the most expensive entree...) A LIBERTY TREE sandwich! Actually, all of the names were neat, but this happened to be a chicken salad sandwich. All of us had the Lentil soup; Justine waited for her Maurice Salad.

I met a lot of concerned people who also had grown tired of the fraud problem. Maybe, just maybe if I kept on trying, I could help the other victims whom were lost and didn't know what their next step would be.

Chapter 23

The Mood Has to Be Perfect

The persistent tug to write was powerful. At times it felt as if I would burst if I didn't take the time to sit down to record events. I'd become uptight and notably aggravated with myself. Occasionally, I'd wake up in the morning and this would be my goal for the day. Then, something out of the blue would pop up and 'out the window' the mood went.

Writing was definitely a mood issue; you're either in the correct frame of mind, or your not. Blame it on writer's block, but I don't think that was it. I think it was because I didn't want to take the time to sit down! I also had to be full of energy because without the extra get up and go—my 'story writing' would drain me, like a battery losing its charge. Sometimes, it felt as if I was falling apart. I told Dennis it was time to 'send me out to pasture' or something. Or better yet, the glue factory.

The stress on occasion seemed insurmountable. I was trying to prepare myself for the outcome, once again. I know this had already been said but it seemed to be a true statement: *the corporations win and "us" little people lose.* I guess that's just the way the ball *usually* bounces. But **I** was refusing to think negatively. How often were appeals turned over anyway?

At times it felt as if I was in battle between good and evil and I'll be the first to admit, I was a little superstitious. There's a numeral that has been a favorite of mine and up until recently I had been seeing it every day. I'd look up at the clock and at the exact minute to see the time '3:33'. I read a few years back that seeing the numeral '333' was good luck and meant that ANGELS were among you, at *that* very moment, and served as a reminder that they are always around. I liked it when I looked up at the clock and would see my favorite time displaying on its face. Especially when I rolled over in bed, in the middle of the night, and the clock was illuminating the room with bright red numbers.

Lately, I haven't viewed my favorite numeral but my least favorite figure. (Which happened to be "66—".) The clock's incapable of displaying such a time, but it seemed to pop up in a fast food line. So, I'd simply order another item. Sounds silly, don't it? I KNEW that angels existed, but it was also nice to be reminded often. At times, I felt as if I was being tested. Never the less, I planned to continue and hoped to find an attorney to assist... if it was the last thing I did...

If the only piece of advice that you follow, after reading this book, is this. #1- Get a copy of your credit report and review it carefully. Then, every year, request an updated version. (This is a pain in the rear, but it could save you a lot of hassle.) #2-DO NOT give *your social security number* to anyone. (At times, that will be an impossible feat, because you won't be able to receive credit or student loans or pretty much anything else.) #3- Be cautious of phone solicitors. And if they ask you for your mother's maiden name, don't give this information out freely either. Unfortunately, there are many types of fraud. The bottom line is, avoid telling callers ___anything___ regarding your personal information.

Chapter 24

"I Didn't Mean to Eavesdrop!"

It was amazing how many people asked me that question. Some of them thought that I was the one who was awarded the 1.5 million dollars. Don't I wish…just think of how many gifts I could buy then! I don't know how they could misunderstand, the news seemed clear when they announced the verdict. Who knows, maybe they only heard part of the announcement. When I'm asked that familiar question, I answer with, "No, but the State of Michigan will."

My friend from the News Herald newspaper left a message on my answering machine days later. (I had a touch of the flu so I waited a little while before returning the call.) I deal with a certain reporter, a female that I trust, who has written several articles on my situation already.

She was planning to write an updated version of my story for the paper. That's great, because if I were going to try to organize a class action lawsuit, I would need the story to continue to grow. How could I help them if I didn't know about them?

I remember when I met with my reporter, right after the verdict was announced originally. I walked into the Heritage building and signed in with the receptionist and explained that I had an appointment. I took a seat on the sofa that sat against the wall in the small waiting area.

As I waited, rather calmly, I overheard a man talking in a room close to me. The walls of this office did not go all the way up but instead were divided by partition panels. It felt wrong eavesdropping but how could I 'not hear' him? His voice carried rather clearly. He sounded slightly excited and when I realized he was talking about me, I laughed to myself. It was weird to be the topic of ones conversation.

I overheard him say, "I have this lady coming in for a photo shoot in a few minutes. Did you see her on television a few nights ago? She took on the DPP and won. She didn't even have an attorney. My mom really liked her. Is she getting the 1.5 million?"

Now, how could I just sit there and not say a word. Instead of being silent, I replied to faceless voice, trying not to shout ,"No…I didn't get the money!" I knew I had to speak loud enough for my voice to carry back to him. Boy, did he sound shocked when his question was answered, out of the blue. He asked me to come closer and said in a surprised tone, "Where are you? Where are you? Come back here, please!"

I stood up and walked past the receptionist window to another set of windows. I immediately recognized a reporter that I worked with years earlier. I called to report an outstanding citizen that we had living in our city. This person is a dear friend of mine, regardless of our age difference. (I believe he just had his eighty-fifth birthday.) He's an artist and expresses himself by oil painting on canvas. He's extremely talented. You should see the painting he made of Jesus and the Last Supper. I must say it is quite impressive. Mr. Thacker was giving me free painting lessons for awhile.

I met the reporter at his home when she went to interview him. See he's deaf. So when the interview began, she asked him the question and I'd quickly write it down so he could read it. Then, Mr. Thacker would answer her audibly. This went on for about forty-five minutes.

The article was more than I imagined. It was a full-page spread with his picture shown and a large "A" for Andrew, which is his first name. This gesture ended up making him a very happy man when the story came out, around Thanksgiving, this one year.

I stopped by at Christmas to exchange gifts with him and he was smiling and visibly pleased. I wanted him to receive recognition for his creativity.

After greeting the reporter that wrote such a wonderful article, a man stood up. He was kneeling on the ground fiddling with his camera. I knew he was the photographer whom I had overheard. He quickly met me in the hall and began asking questions. Shortly thereafter, we moved into a rather large conference room surrounded by more blue partition walls.

Sitting on the conference table was an 'old time' rotary phone. I thought to myself, "oh my, they're going to make me pretend to talk into it…I'm going to look and feel silly!" The phone had to be older than I was!

The interview went on for about thirty minutes and then I had to pose with the relic. Of course I felt ridiculous and I KNOW I'm not photogenic...in the least. Sometimes, if the picture is candid, the photo turns out okay. I don't know why that is. If I know that I'm being photographed, I must act different or *something*.

I had to pretend to talk into the black, heavy phone. I had forgotten how heavy one of those old fashioned phones were. Now with the convenience of the cordless phone, I couldn't even imagine being tied down to one spot. It was so heavy it could be used as a weapon!

Chapter 25

I Found An Attorney!

I had a consultation appointment with an attorney who had agreed to take the time to meet with me. Most importantly, if he found out that **we had a case,** he would consider a class action lawsuit.

I packed up all of my papers, three cases worth in all, and drove to Farmington Hills to meet Mr. Barry Seifman and Mr. Ray Gazelle. I'm going to be quite frank here, my initial opinion was "this isn't going to work."

I didn't care for either of them, at first. I know I'm extremely sensitive, no one has to tell me that fact. I mean, every night at the dinner table, when I was around the age of four or five, I'd spill my milk. I don't mean occasionally, but it seemed like I spilled the darn glass of milk **every single night**.

My dad never hollered at me...all he did was raise his left eyebrow to form an inverted V. This look sent me bawling, running off down the hallway, to my room. (Luckily, mom had only poured me a tiny glass.) To top it off, the spilled liquid *always* seemed to head in my dad's direction, like his lap. Thus, giving me the nick-name, 'The Little Dumper.'

After a minute or two of me acting a fool, I'd be called back to the dinner table. I'd return to a slightly damp table and somewhere would lay a few saturated dishtowels. I'd be forced back to continue dinner with the family. And every time this happened, I'd return with the 'snubbing' sound. (You know how someone talks after they've hyperventilated and begin the 'sort- of' hiccup breathing.) He'd tell me, "Stop that snubbing…it's okay." So that pretty much tells you how big of a crybaby I was. Although, I would hope that the last thirty–some years has made me into something other than 'the little dumper.'

Now, back to the attorney story, before I was distracted by the 'milk' incident.

I do not like to be told to be quiet, but it is sometimes needed. When I'm excited, or nervous, I can begin to sound like a broken record (for those of you aren't familiar with records, when one has a flaw on it, like a scratch, it will repeat itself continuously, until someone moves the needle.)

Well, during our first meeting, I was told to be quiet, I don't know how *many* times. I was asked to tell my story, *briefly*. Well, how in the heck can I tell a five-year story in two minutes? Not possible! Besides, I hate to be told to shut up! I think the request was more like, "Quit wandering off to a different subject." They weren't different subjects, the same subject, and only different parts of it. One must remember that this had been going on for years.

Actually, I thought they were rather rude and abrupt. I tried to keep in mind that attorneys **have to be hard**, or else they would not perform well in court, under pressure.

I obeyed and was quiet and didn't speak until spoken too. No, I didn't cry, I'm not four anymore. (Although, my feelings were hurt and I came close to getting up and walking out.)

I answered with short quick answers, when asked a question. Thinking back on it, I'm quite confident that my arms were crossed—a sure sign that I'm perturbed. The questions that were asked of me ranged from all sorts, from my previous jobs, past experiences to finances.

More than once, I felt stupid, because the dates were not clear in my mind. I had notes to refer too, but of course, the questions asked weren't the ones on my cheat sheet. I certainly did not feel comfortable. Then, it dawned on me; could they be possibly testing me? Maybe they wanted to see if I had what it took to stand trial. If they could get me to stutter and screw up then the cross-examiner would be able to also. It was if they were purposely trying to ruffle my feathers. Well, they succeeded in doing such. My feathers were more than ruffled...more like coming out.

After the end of our interview, they agreed to investigate. So I must not have been that annoying after all. We shook hands and I was told to call, anytime, if I had questions or worries. To be quite honest, I really didn't want to talk to them. I dislike feeling belittled.

P.K. Nelski

Luckily things changed and I began to like both Barry and Ray. Together, they have already been a great deal of help to me. Barry even met me in Detroit the day that I was presented with the 'Consumer of the Year' Award. (Just incase I was hounded by reporters or something.)

So, to make a long story short, they have agreed to take the case, on a contingent basis. My dream was finally coming true! I now had an attorney! Almost six years later, I had accomplished that task. By the way, they seemed very aggressive. I don't have to light a fire under them to get them moving. I have made a good choice, I just know it.

I can't reveal too much about the pending legal action. A few of the newspapers called and interviewed me for an updated status and announced the possible class action lawsuit. My attorney began getting calls from others requesting assistance soon after the news announced the story.

The paperwork on my case was filed, rather quickly, since the Statue of Limitations was about to expire. My case is pending further developments and I am pleased that we are moving forward.

I soon grew tired of people ridiculing me for settling for such a small monetary figure. I was awarded for *some* of my time and expenses. On the bright side, the DPP was fined the 1.5 Million, awarded to the State, that is, if the appeal goes our way. I can't tell you how many times I've heard, "man, you're crazy for settling for that amount…you should have been awarded the million!"

For me to say my life would have been stress free, without the fraud scam, I would be lying. Does anyone have a picture perfect life? No. *BUT*, stating that the 'extra' problems *made life that much harder...* **is the truth**!

I'm not sure how much writing I'll be doing in the next few weeks. Dennis went to the hospital to have biopsies taken of his Prostate. He had been watching his PSA level closely and had noticed an increase over the last few years. We now had to wait for the results. He's not that old, only forty-six. The biopsies are probably just routine.

The next few chapters have nothing to do with fraud, except for the fact that I devoted virtually no time to the subject. My attorney's knew that I had my own personal struggles to face and our communication continued, but not as aggressively. So, even though the next few pages are not of identity theft nature, they are very important to me.

Chapter 26

Things Hit Hard

Dennis and I called for the test results on the biopsies, but the doctor wasn't in and the nurse refused to give them to us. This didn't make me feel too good. Now we had to wait through the weekend. The kicker was this, the results were in front of her, but the doctor had a rule, test results were to be handled personally, by him. Wait, wait, and more waiting.

The following Monday, the call came in and I had a funny feeling. The strange thing about this was, prior to this phone call, I really thought he was fine. On a scale of '1-10', of worry, I was at scoring this as a '3'. I walked the phone out to Dennis; he was working in the 'Out building.'(Our large metal building where he keeps equipment.) I handed the phone to him and he began the conversation with his physician. But instead of talking, he was mostly listening.

Mariah, our dog was outside with us too, so I played with her while I patiently waited the results. I knew something was wrong because Dennis wouldn't look into my eyes. I kept trying to get his attention but he kept diverting his attention elsewhere and seemed to be turning away from me. He didn't want to look at me for some reason.

He finally hung up the phone and told me the news. Out of the ten biopsies they took, seven were malignant. My much-loved husband had Prostate Cancer. It was his birthday and he had just turned forty-seven, what a birthday gift. When he said the words, "I have Cancer, seven out of ten spots are malignant," I immediately broke down and began to sob. My head was spinning and I felt like I was in a dream, or a nightmare, praying I would wake up. Eventually, I could no longer hold my body up and fell to my knees. Could it be a mistake? Did someone read the tests wrong? His PSA level was 3.3—3.5. Most doctors don't recommend biopsies until the level is, at least, 4. (Oh yea, they do not want to order the PSA test until the patient is fifty years old.) If Dennis had waited another three or four years, his moderate growing cancer could have possibly spread to other parts of his body and cost him his life.

I stood up and began to walk up the gravel driveway that led to the house and I fell again. I thought to myself, "I NEED HIM! I LOVE HIM! I've finally found someone who loves me, with all of his heart, and he has CANCER!" I've never experienced this feeling before—I could not hold my body upright. My knees felt like they were made of rubber.

Dennis picked me up and supported my weight into the house. Once inside, my chest began to tighten up. I couldn't tell if it was my heart or if I was having a nervous breakdown or what. I immediately got on the phone and called Doctor Go and left him a message. Within, what seemed like seconds, the call was returned.

I said, " Doctor Go...Dennis has Prostate Cancer!" I was out of control and I wasn't sure if he could understand me, because as I said before, I stutter when I cry. (Did it when I was three and I guess I still do it now.)

He said, "Calm down, Patricia. You need to **calm down**. Listen to me! Prostate Cancer has a high cure rate, especially when diagnosed at an early stage. Things will be okay."

I replied with, "I think I'm having a nervous breakdown, or something. I can hardly breathe, my chest hurts and I have a migraine headache! I don't know how much more I can handle." I seriously thought I was having a nervous breakdown, although I don't have a clue as to what one feels like.

My doctor knows me well, thank God. He sternly told me to go take my medications. Prior to this, he had prescribed several mild drugs, to help manage my situations. One was given to control my migraine headaches and the other is to calm me down.

It seemed as if I had been on this HUGE, ROLLER COASTER OF LIFE for **so** long. And believe me, I was ready to get off of the ride for awhile. Stress, stress and more stress.

Doctor Go assured me that it was normal for me to 'freak out' when hearing those awful words. He said if I didn't react; now that would be abnormal. As usual, he helped me through that first awful hour. He knew how much I cared for Dennis and I'm not sure if I could go on without him.

In all honesty, my husband is the one who inspired me to write this book. After all of the phone calls that flooded our home, he too realized that there were a lot of people needing help. Any advice from one who had been down the path was helpful. I often said that I was "dropping this fraud thing" and he'd answer with, "You'll regret it Pat. Life has to go on." (And it's certainly any writer's dream to see their work in print.)

I told Doctor Go that Dennis's birthday party was to take place in two hours and I had to go make a hundred meatballs. (Now, that was an over exaggeration, I only planned on making thirty or so.) I had a headache as big as a house, but I didn't want to cancel his party. I had already made the Pineapple Upside Down cake, Brownies and Banana Nut Bread.

I called Subway and I asked for a five- foot party sub. The guy was really nice and said I could have it tomorrow. Tomorrow? What good would it do me tomorrow? I started to cry again and I explained the situation. He immediately changed the plan. Instead of the party sub he suggested twenty, twelve- inch submarine sandwiches. I agreed and he had them ready for me in half an hour.

When I went to pick them up, he made up separate containers of each of the toppings. (Like black olives, sweet peppers, onions, green peppers, lettuce, everything needed, even bags of condiments.) The manager insisted on carrying everything out to my car for me.

The family showed up for the party and we tried to act as normal as possible. You could feel the apprehensiveness around the room. No one knew exactly what to say. Eric, Dennis's son came with the grand babies. Thank

God for those beautiful children. Madison is three and the twins, Megan and Morgan will be two in a few months. There's not much time to sit around and cry when you have grand babies needing attention and running in all different directions.

The party went okay, although I did cry. So did my sister. I was in a sort-of *fog* or state of disbelief. My parents were there for us, once again. Tracy, a dear friend of mine, worked at the hospital and I called her that evening, after the party. She wasn't home, so I left her a message on her answering machine. I'm not sure what I said, or how desperate I sounded, but she returned the call, early the following morning. She asked me to keep her posted on when Dennis would be at the hospital.

I also called Subway, the next morning, and offered a thank you. I *promised* to give them all of my submarine sandwich business, from then on.

Tests were scheduled to see if the Cancer had spread to other parts of his body. One was the day after his birthday; the other was going to have to wait, almost a week, since the department was booked.

The first test, Dennis had to go to alone. I know I should have been there for him but I didn't get out of bed that day, except to use the restroom. (And to call Subway.) I was very depressed and had a kicking sore throat. (Oh, the migraine was also present.)

Doctor Go called and was surprised to hear my raspy, almost completely inaudible, voice and decided that I needed an antibiotic. He said that Dennis and I were on his mind and he wanted to make sure that we were dealing with the news. It was kind of him to take the time to call and check up on the both of us. I know one thing for sure; Dr. Go is truly ***one in a million.***

My husband feels fortunate to have been under the care of Dr. Go. A group health care provider covers Dennis and we all know how picky they can be with all of their rules, referrals and protocol guidelines. Dr. Go stood back for a moment and took a look at the entire picture. The family history of Prostate Cancer was first considered and the rise in Dennis's PSA level. He then decided that further testing was warranted. We certainly owe him a big thank you. I think he stuck his neck out, going against the 'normal' and following his gut instinct.

Tracy is pretty special too. Somehow, the test that was scheduled for the following week was moved up to the next day. (I guess there was a last minute cancellation.) So, I pulled myself together and drove with Dennis to the hospital for the CAT scan.

Once at the hospital, we were asked to take a seat in the hallway, on the bench, to wait until the procedure room became vacant. Out of the blue, a woman came up to us and looked directly at me and asked, "Dear child, what are you having done today?" I must have looked like a complete wreck! —She seemed surprised when I explained that we were there for my husband. It was obvious that he was handling this better than I was. From that point on, I decided that I would have to just straighten up and once again, lean on my faith.

With Tracy's pull, the tests were not only complete, but also read before the upcoming weekend. Thank God. The Cancer was contained within the Prostate Gland.

Dennis called his sister, Sheryl, who had been a nurse for many years, at the University of Michigan. She recommended an excellent physician, who was not only an Urologist, but an Oncologist too.

Surgery was scheduled and was to take place in two months. We decided it was best to have the entire Prostate removed. And the sooner the better, before the Cancer had a chance to break apart and travel elsewhere in his body.

I had already placed Dennis in the hands of God, knowing that somehow he'd get us through this. I had to become strong, for Dennis's sake, and be a shoulder for him to lean on, instead of the other way around.

My battle over identity theft was placed on hold. Obviously, this was no longer my focus. I didn't feel like I could handle any more than the current problem, since I was spread pretty thin BEFORE the 'C-Word' entered our lives. My energy was going to be saved to help my husband get well again.

We were sitting on the couch, one night, and I laid my hand on his stomach and shut my eyes. With all of my might, I tried to picture a healing power coming from me. (I didn't know if it would work, but what the heck, I'd try anything to make him better.) I hadn't noticed that he stopped watching T.V, but instead was focused on me. He said, "Honey, are you praying for me?" I replied, "I most certainly am!" He smiled and simply said, "Thank you..."

Chapter 27

The Surgery is Over...
Prognosis is Good!

My mom and dad met me at the hospital and sat in the waiting room with me while the surgery was being performed. I trusted Dennis's Urologist completely, but there was always that chance of something going wrong or something else discovered, once the incision was made.

Truly, I was a nervous wreck and I'm glad my parents were there for me, once again. I took a mild medication, for my nerves and tried to relax during the scheduled three- hour surgery.

Even though I stated that the identity theft battle was on hold, I still brought along with me my manuscript to look over. I tried to edit and proofread my book, but my mind was clearly not focused on what was now 'on the back burner'. My husband's health was the number ONE concern.

My mother-in-law suggested that I take my needle-point, to try to divert my worrying elsewhere. (She gave me a large tablecloth with tons of embroidery thread a year ago. I wasn't big on needlepoint, so needless to say the tablecloth had a long way to go.)

I threaded the needle and began to work on my craft project. My mom was getting a little worried when I almost stuck her with the needle during one of my long sewing strides. Then, I poked my finger, not once, but three times and drew blood.

My mom suggested that I put it away because my stitches were not coming out so good. On the other hand, I thought that this was a perfect time to knock a dent in the table cloth, since I swore that I'd have it done within a year.

After stabbing myself in the finger numerous times and almost putting my mother's eye out, I lost the needle in the carpet of the waiting room. I thought for sure that someone was going to get hurt on it, so I got down on my hands and knees, looking foolish, until I found it. I still refused to give up, that is until I goofed and sewed the edge of the material, smack—dab, to the middle of the tablecloth.

The three-hour procedure ended up lasting over four hours. I was thankful when our doctor appeared and informed us that Dennis was out of surgery. He said that it went well and that it was a 'pleasure to operate on him.' I can imagine that it would be more pleasant (?) to operate on a well-toned individual instead of someone who was overweight.

We were fortunate to have been able to get the test results, had met with an excellent surgeon and have the operation completed, all within two months. (Two months to this exact day, as a matter of fact.) I **know** God was on our side.

The appeal process is underway and I don't doubt that this will end up taking some time. The civil suit has been started and it's way too early to speculate the outcome of that subject. I've considered lobbying for new laws. I'll be checking into that, in the near future.

Chapter 28

My Heart Is Broken, Along With the Rest of our Nation

September 11th, 2001 was a tragic day that will forever remain imbedded in my memory. Dennis and I woke up that morning by a call from his son, Eric, informing us that one of the World Trade Center buildings had just been struck by a passenger airplane.

We got up and turned on the news. The image of the plane colliding into the high rise structure sent chills through my body and immediate tears to my eyes. It was as if it was not real…but an awful reenactment from a movie.

The first thought that entered my mind was, could this be an accident? My chills refused to go away. The broadcast on television echoed throughout our home. I was making Dennis breakfast but could still hear the news commentaries informing the public that another passenger jet was high jacked and was heading for it's twin tower.

(I didn't plan on involving another subject into this book, but how can I avoid it?)

I was wondering what was next on the terrorist list? Strangely enough, Dennis and I had planned on taking a trip to Las Vegas, possibly on September 11th, but our tickets came through a few days late. The tickets now lay on the coffee table, in the living room, for God only knows how long since I was now amongst the majority of the people who are afraid to fly. Hopefully, this will pass with time—especially when that's exactly what the terrorists want us to be—afraid. What could I do to make a difference for all of the sadness that surrounds me?

I guess you could say that I was in the state of shock. If I felt that sad, how did the people living around ground zero feel? How about the ones who were missing loved ones? My heart was so heavy with grief, trying to deal with the overwhelming frustration, knowing that there was nothing I could do to help.

On my thirty-seventh birthday, I stood on the corner of a busy intersection, with my husband; collecting money for New York's Fallen Hero's. Dennis is a Lieutenant on the fire department and has approximately one year before he can retire. His entire department worked together and raised over Thirty Thousand dollars in one afternoon! The generosity was a comfort to see.

The tears of others met my tears while they sat at the red light that I was begging at. I must have touched over one hundred hands in a three-hour period. I would say 'thank you' for the donation and the response was, "No...THANK YOU!" I only collected $250.00, but I can honestly say that this was the most rewarding way to spend my birthday. I finally felt as if I had done something. (I prayed continually.)

I hope this book, that I have poured my heart and soul into, will be read and can benefit someone along their way. I must admit, it seems **trivial** , and *is trivial*, compared to what America is now facing. The last thing I will say, and I will end this book, to begin another. <u>FRAUD is FRAUD</u>. Fake identities are FRAUD. The pilots that hi-jacked our own airplanes were imposters. My identity theft is insignificant, but shows that it is happening ALL AROUND US.

Our nation has many problems to overcome and the first and foremost is to send out the message that we, as PROUD AMERICANS, will fight back. Our forefathers, who founded this great country, had to fight for freedom and independence and we will continue to follow their footsteps with renewed determination.

President Bush has impressed me. See, I did not vote for him. But I can honestly say that he has **won me over**. When he recited the 23rd Psalm...my heart melted. I am thankful he is using God in his message to our nation. We need God, not just now, in our time of despair, but for all encounters in life.

Epilogue

I'm not sure when justice will be served in my dilemma. I can say one thing for sure; others will have to answer for all of the wrong doings, one day, in one way or another.

Perhaps, I will lobby for new laws that will protect us from fraud. This will be a long battle, but I'll find the strength again. For now, I must focus on doing something to help the victims and families that have been torn apart by this terrible disaster.

I still believe that justice will be served, in more than one way. I will continue to pray, with all of my being, that this will be so.

<u>GOD BLESS AMERICA</u>!

The following few pages were an earlier attempt of mine, to **try** to help others clear their name of identity theft. (This was written before I testified in Lansing.) I hung up flyers, trying to solicit the information on bulletin boards all over town, hoping others would see them. A few inquired, but not as many as I had hoped for. Now, I will share these pages with you. Maybe some of the information will be useful.

$ Restoring *YOUR* Credit! $
By: P.K. Nelski

Have you been a victim of credit card fraud? Have you recently been denied credit and you're not sure why? Maybe you should check and see what your credit report looks like. I inquired about my report and was shocked!

I knew something was wrong, since I had been getting calls from creditors, demanding that I pay my bills. The damage that was done to my name was tremendous and this was accomplished by using **MY** social security number and a forged signature!

I should have known something was going on, because at one point, I was receiving so many pre-approved applications, from banks that I have never heard of. (This revealed to me that my credit was excellent, at one point. Then all of the sudden, they stopped.)

With only a signature, and **your** social security number, someone can open an account, **in your name!** Security needs to be tightened up when it comes to the availability of social security numbers. But no one seemed to care! (A lot of places like schools and banks, use social security numbers as account numbers or for identification purposes.) Don't they realize how confidential a social security number should be?

Five years ago, I was a victim of credit card fraud. I was harassed continually from creditors, with calls coming in as late as nine o'clock at night or even on Sunday afternoons! Even after telling them that I was not the one who opened up the account, they still called me daily. I was in the middle of a nightmare. My excellent credit was turned up side down, in what seemed like, overnight! The initial shock sent me from feeling upset, to the point of tears——then to anger! How could somebody cause so much damage, in such a short period of time?

I called many attorneys, asking for help. None of them were interested in taking my case. It was up to me to get the ball rolling. I had to be the one who made the initial contact with the creditors. **IF**, the charges still remained, then I could possibly seek legal action.

The process to clear my name has been a long, tedious haul. I was able to restore my credit, to its original state, and you can too!

The first step is to write to the credit reporting agencies, and request a copy of your credit report. You will need to send a copy of your Driver's license along with your request. If you do not have one, they will accept a utility bill, as long the bill is in your name. You will also have to provide your social security number.

There are three major credit-reporting agencies in the United States. (So if you hire the services of a small credit agency, they are just tapping into one of the three major agencies.) The following addresses that follow should be accurate—they were taken from my documents.

Experian
701 Experian Parkway
Allen, TX 75013
1-800-583-4080

Transunion
2 Baldwin Place
Chester, PA 19022
1-800-888-4213

Equifax
P.O. Box 105069
Atlanta, GA 30348
1-800-290-8749

After you get your report, look it over carefully. Take the time to learn what the different codes mean. You'll need to learn to read the report to understand what it is telling you. The report will tell you if the account is delinquent and by how many days. It will reveal how long the account has been active and if payments were late or missed altogether. Information usually stays on your report for a period of seven years, unless you file a certain type of bankruptcy, which remains on your report for a period of ten years.

You are entitled, by law, to the information in your file that has been used against you. You can dispute the inaccurate data, and it must be corrected or deleted. You may seek damages from the violators, if they do not comply.

The SECOND STEP is to compose a letter, addressing it to the bank that the account is drawn from. Inform them in your letter, that the Account is a fraudulent account, not opened yourself. (Be sure to include the account number in your correspondence.) Ask them to send you an Affidavit of Forgery and Fraud. (This is a written Declaration of Oath—stating that you were a victim of fraud.) You'll need to contact a Notary of Republic and fill out the form in the presence of the Notary. Usually the city in which you reside will employ a notary. When you are composing your letter to the bank to inform them of the fraudulent activity, you'll need to notify <u>the three credit reporting agencies also</u>.

After you have notified the creditor, they have the right to conduct an investigation. This investigation could take up to 60 days. In this time frame, the creditor should notify the credit-reporting agency of the error. The information should then be removed. If they still refuse to remove the inaccurate data, get legal advice from an attorney. (This part didn't help me, but maybe with the changing of the times, it will help you.) You may also contact the Federal Trade Commission. The address is listed below.

FEDERAL TRADE COMMISSION
CONSUMER RESPONSE CENTER—FCA
600 Pennsylvania Ave., NW
WASHINGTON, DC 20580
1-202-382-4357

MAKE PHOTOCOPIES of all of your documents. KEEP A GOOD PAPER TRAIL! A spiral notebook is an important asset in keeping track of the events that take place. I look back on my journals often.

Keep in mind that bad entries on your report could keep you from obtaining that loan, mortgage——or in even in purchasing a car! The first credit report that I reviewed was twenty pages long, when a normal report should only consist of two or three pages. Your report will include the names of different organizations that have recently requested your credit information. (A potential employer or a credit card firm wanting to extend you a line of credit.) Make sure all of the information on your report is correct. Are the previous addresses correct? How about past employers? It's your report, so it should be **right.**

You are entitled to one free report every twelve months upon request if you certify that you are unemployed and are seeking employment, or if you are on welfare. If you have been denied credit, or have been a victim of fraud, you may also request copies until the problem is cleared up.

If one agency has information on you, most likely they all three have it. If you find that you HAVE been a victim of fraud, you'll need to communicate with all of the agencies, until each of them has done their job and restored your credit to it's original state. Be prepared, this will be time consuming. If you're in the process of taking a major financial step, the inaccurate data could slow down the qualifying process of getting a loan.

Any correspondence should be sent out as certified mail, then you will have proof that you mailed the document. It is probable that someday you will need the documentation. (Unfortunately these costs add up.)

To protect yourself from additional fraudulent activity, you may want to write to the credit reporting agencies requesting that they add a "Fraud Victim Statement" to your report. Then a "red flag" goes up, making it impossible for anyone to use **your** social security number. Keep in mind that this will also make it difficult for YOU to open new lines of credit. You will need to speak directly to the credit-reporting agency to identify yourself, before credit will be granted. This is an **important step** to prevent the criminal from striking again!

<u>Here are the steps to follow:</u>

1. Request your credit report, and look it over carefully.
2. Highlight the fraudulent charges, or the ones in question.
3. Make sure all of the data is correct, like previous addresses and employers.
4. Compose two basic letters. One to the bank that holds the fraudulent account and send the other to all three credit-reporting agencies.
5. Make photocopies of the letters, and mail it them out— "REGISTERED MAIL".
6. After receiving the affidavit, call your city to locate a notary—-get the document notarized. Once again, make photocopies.

Wait a month or two. Soon, you should start to receive information regarding the pending investigation.

8. Request another copy of your credit report. If the charges have not been removed, even **after** completing the Affidavit, you have two choices:

   A. Notify them **again**, demanding the information be removed or you will be forced to seek legal action.

OR

   B. If you have already notified them several times, and have supporting documentation, consider seeking legal action.

I suggest that you periodically check your report, and obtain a current copy approximately every twelve months. GOOD LUCK to you!

I'm learning to take it one day at a time. I am currently working with my two attorneys and just got off of the phone with an attorney from Washington. (An attorney from Federal Trade Commission.) When the FCRA was written, it was basically written to correct inaccuracies, not fraudulent activity. Identity theft is a whole new breed of problems. Truthfully, the current Fair Credit Reporting Act offers little consumer protection.

There is not
<u>ONE</u> LAW GOVERNING IDENTITY THEFT!

I wonder what my next step will be from here? I'll continue to try to take it one day at a time. Maybe I'll lobby for new laws, maybe I'll re-write parts of my autobiography and publish that next. Much of my time is spent wondering about our future. As long as we stand United, there is strength in numbers and when there is faith, anything is possible.

Don't ever give up, if you believe!

"The Billboard." Corresponds to chapter 21. When I was driving, while deep in thought, I looked up and saw this billboard.

Eric, Melissa, Amanda, and Kirk.

My parents, John and Jean Whitaker.

Dennis, my husband, John and Lillian Nelski, Eric
with his wife Sharon. Eric's holding one twin,
Megan and Sharon's holding the other, Morgan.
Madison is standing in the front.

Shirley, my sister-in-law, helping me brainstorm
with ideas.

Laurie, my sister, who gave me confidence and she's holding Mariah, my pooch.